SOUNDING THE ICEBERG

An Essay on Canadian Historical Novels

DENNIS DUFFY

ECW PRESS

CANADIAN CATALOGUING IN PUBLICATION DATA

Duffy, Dennis, 1938–
    Sounding the iceberg : an essay on Canadian
historical novels

Bibliography: p.
Includes index.
ISBN 0-920763-13-8 (bound). — ISBN 0-920763-24-6
(pbk.)

1. Historical fiction, Canadian (English)–History and
criticism. * 2. Historical fiction, Canadian (French)–
History and criticism. * 3. History in literature.
I. Title.

PS8191.H5D83 1986   C813'.009'358   C86–093272–9
PR9192.6.H5D83 1986

Sounding the Iceberg has been published with the help of a grant from
the Canadian Federation for the Humanities, using funds provided by the
Social Sciences and Humanities Research Council of Canada. Additional
grants have been provided by the Ontario Arts Council and The Canada
Council.

Designed by The Dragon's Eye Press; typeset by Ideagraphics, Oakville,
Ontario; printed by Hignell Printing, Winnipeg, Manitoba.

Published by ECW PRESS, 307 Coxwell Avenue, Toronto, Ontario M4L 3B5.

ACKNOWLEDGEMENTS

This book has been published with the help of a grant from the Canadian Federation for the Humanities, using funds provided by the Social Sciences and Humanities Research Council of Canada. I am grateful for their aid, and for the sound advice on the manuscript tendered me by two anonymous appraisers the Federation provided.

Mr. Al Purdy kindly consented to my use of his work for the title and epigraph of this study. The University of Toronto gave me a year of administrative leave during which this essay was written, while the Principal's Office of Innis College provided funds for the final stages of preparation.

Professors Peter Allen, W. J. Keith, and Elizabeth Waterston commented helpfully on an early version of a section of this text. My daughter Elaine provided valuable aid in indexing and verification. Messrs. Jack David and Robert Lecker proved themselves speedy and supportive publishers. Ms. Edna Barker performed painful and beneficial stylistic surgery. This book's dedicatee came up with the best version of a title. Thanks to all who have helped. Not they, but I am the architect of the book's flaws.

FOR MARY ANN

Contents

" . . . the Canadian past. All those numberless people who preceded us, the shadows in our brains who made us real and thereby became fictional themselves. Dressed in their odd clothes, with fixed unnatural expressions, they stare backward in time. The universe in our own heads somehow fails to include them, despite the logic of our knowing they once existed, as we now exist and eventually shall disappear as they have disappeared into nowhere. The oddness, the strange differences between then and now sometimes give you a feeling that here we are, the warm, living and visible tip of a cold invisible dead iceberg below the surface of time."

Al Purdy, "Life with Father," *Books in Canada*, Dec. 1984, p. 22

Introduction

EVEN FICTIONAL CHARACTERS read historical novels. A certain Mabel Clint used "Harold Saxon" as her pen name when she wrote a book called *Under the King's Bastion. A Romance of Quebec* in 1902. The pseudonym suggests too intense a reading of *Ivanhoe* and *Hereward the Wake*, and the book is little more than a fictionalized tourist guide to the city of Quebec. Clint's heroine evades a fortune hunter by stopping at every location in Quebec City that has ever had a postcard made of it, and Clint's fortune hunter sallies forth in search of his prey carrying a book, William Kirby's 1877 historical novel, *The Golden Dog*. In the course of the action, other historical novels are mentioned, such as McLennan and McIlwraith's *The Span O' Life* (1899) and Sir Gilbert Parker's widely known *The Seats of the Mighty* (1896). Later, Clint's rascal appears carrying the final volume of Francis Parkman's monumental history of France in North America, *Montcalm and Wolfe* (1884). Parkman's prose epic, which appeared in 1851, gave English-speaking readers their first romantic glimpse of the grandeur of New France and the epic of its conquest. Mabel Clint, whatever her failings as a novelist, well knew the key works that would help her grasp imaginatively Canadian space and time.

Nearly forty years after Clint used *The Golden Dog* as a Vergilian token offering the traveller admission to another world, another writer employed a similar motif. A character in Mazo de la Roche's *Whiteoak Heritage* (1940) reads from a copy of Kirby's work while strolling about the Citadel. *The Golden Dog* fascinated another of de la Roche's characters, the poet Eden Whiteoak. One of his projects was to write about "the loves of Bigot," as we are told in *Finch's Fortune* (1931). This fascination with a romanticized past was shared by Eden's creator: de la Roche wrote a history, *Quebec: Historic Seaport* (1944), which squeezed from the storied stones their every lush association.

The writers and readers of Canadian historical novels were not taken seriously by critics, and the books stand in unread rows, dusty potboilers punctuated by the odd engaging romance. The classic discussion of them in Canadian letters remains a distanced one. It indicates that while such work cannot be excluded from any bill of lading for our cultural cargo, it does not make up our most dazzling merchandise.[1] The 1983 *Oxford Companion to Canadian Literature* has entries on "Travel Literature in English" and "Prairie Writing," but nothing about historical fiction. Yet our most successful fiction writer at the turn of the century had reached the top largely by writing historical novels. The best-seller successes of a Gilbert Parker could hold no lasting claim on critical intelligences today. His works were often melodramatic, and were adorned with baroque plots and ornate dialogue. It took great effort to drag Canadian literature into the codes of literary modernism, and few works of fiction dealt with what critics consider serious matters. No one had time to waste on historical fiction. By the 1930s, "serious fiction" meant works in which realistic conventions of narrative exploit non-heroic characters and situations. Such fiction employed symbolic and associative patterns; historical fiction contained nationalist quasi-allegories about Canada's destiny. University course outlines canonize work as grey as Sinclair Ross's *As for Me and My House*; they do not revel in the grand opera of *The Seats of the Mighty*.

In the 1930s, two serious writers, Philip Child and Léo-Paul Desrosiers, produced historical novels, but their ventures were treated as sideshows. Child's *The Village of Souls* could be viewed as a dream-like romance inserted into a Canadian historical setting. Desrosiers held a place in French-Canadian letters similar to the one Thomas Raddall would hold in English-Canadian fiction. None of the three writers produced pot-boilers, but they did deal with the kind of extroverted world that attracts historical novelists. In such a world, our interior dispositions are less important than the exterior world's molding and curtailment of them. The modern novel is more preoccupied with the inner world, and the extroversion of historical novels forms a steep barrier to serious consideration. Indeed, as my discussion of *Kamouraska* will indicate, a historical novel with inner preoccupations will not be treated as a historical novel by critics, who find a discussion of the psychological more congenial. All historical novels discuss collective processes in one form or another. The trick to producing a good one is in the successful handling of both inward and outward matters, in producing characters at once convincing in themselves and yet representative of larger tendencies.

Whatever the barriers to critical appreciation of the genre, by the 1970s, a number of works appeared that placed historical fiction squarely in our literary mainstream. *Kamouraska, The Temptations of Big Bear, The Wars, Perpetual Motion* and a host of lesser and hybrid works proved impossible to ignore. That impossibility compelled me to attempt this study. What I have attempted here is something in the nature of a pointed survey. The use of historical settings and themes by some of our finest writers is a fact. To see this fact as nothing more than the outcome of a series of random factors places more faith in chance than I am willing to grant. Writers like Rudy Wiebe, Timothy Findley, Anne Hébert, and Graeme Gibson do not pull their works out of hats. Something inherent in the nature of the historical fiction must be calling forth their highest powers. To show how this has come about, I offer a story of how the historical novel in Canada moved from a popular and revered form, to a merely popular one, and then finally to its position among the serious fiction of our time. My gaze is not steady. Not every novel, nor every writer, nor every novel by every writer, attracts my attention. Someone's landmark is bound to have escaped my search. Some works of slight interest from the viewpoint of form and technique attract more attention than those with greater claims in this area. All this seems the inevitable result of attempting to cut a critical path.

As with any historical narrative, this one, too, is a fiction. It imposes an after–the–fact teleology and an assumed inter-relationship upon discrete literary events. It gathers a series of phenomena into a progress, discerning a beginning, middle and end to a process that in actual fact seems removed from such a weight of intentionality. The results of this argument prove no less a fiction than the works examined during its course. I can only hope that my fitting of things into a pattern appears to the reader as a series of gentle nudges rather than a ham-fisted shove. The alternative to this pattern-making would have been the creation of a list, and those we have.

The urge to deliver something more than a series of catalogue entries also demanded categorical exclusions. Canadian writers have achieved international popularity by writing stories based on other people's histories: for example, Thomas B. Costain and Pauline Gedge. Other people's writers have dealt famously with our history, as works of Willa Cather, Kenneth Roberts and James Fenimore Cooper suggest. I will discuss works written by Canadians about Canada. The study of nationalist themes holds together the many beads on this string. Literary currents spill over national floodwalls. Anyone attempting to assess the popularity of historical fiction during the middle of this century would have to pay closer attention to *Gone With the Wind* or H. F. M. Prescott's *The Man on a Donkey* than to any Canadian text. I leave that cosmopolitan story to others. I have divided my argument into three parts, based upon chronology. The first takes the form from its beginnings to its romantic apogee in *The Seats of the Mighty*. The second deals with a plethora of works written during the next six decades, and discusses the unfolding of the form's potential in such writers as Desrosiers, Child, Robert Laroque De Roquebrune, Thomas Raddall, and Louis Vaczek. The final part deals primarily with the contemporaries I have mentioned. My argument and method of selection stem from a conviction about the broad contours of a particular Canadian literary enterprise. Both theoretical and specific treatments of historical fiction abound.[2] They provide a sense of the philosophical and cultural predispositions of historical works, but leave the practical critic with the job of setting forth a definition of the subject. The alternative to this is the creation of a piece of structuralist theorizing that picks certain literary objects as points in its argument, a step I have resolutely avoided. It is already being undertaken by sensibilities more congenial to it than mine.[3]

I consider historical novels as those set, to a great extent, within a past with which the reader has no direct acquaintance and in which some view of that period appears to be part of the novel's theme. Strictly speaking, most fiction remains historical in its setting. It is located in some past, perhaps a very recent one but a past nonetheless. The childhood of the adult narrator, the hero's family background (as is the case with the made-for-television saga so popular now), the experiences of the parental generation, all provide obvious examples of the historical aspects of present-day settings. The historical novel, on the other hand, emphasizes overtly or implicitly the otherness of that past. This is more a matter of attitude than of a count of years. For example, when Sir Walter Scott founded the genre in 1814 with *Waverley*, he gave his work the subtitle, " 'Tis Sixty Years Since." The subtitle points in two directions. "*Only* sixty years ago, the kind of feudal society found in this book cast its last throw in the Scottish Highlands." An equally valid reading is, "It has been all of sixty years since this happened; the whole business is really dead now." The point is that sixty years have formed a chasm that separates the world of the characters from that of their audience. The end result of a novel like Scott's may be the assertion of a moral continuity between audience and characters. This is the theme of most historical fiction written for children: "Our ancestors worked through their problems with courage and grit, and we'll do the same with the new ones that we face." Many of the novels discussed here will assert that continuity. Yet the reader's initial impression from a work of historical fiction ought to be that of discontinuity. The reader is somewhere different, stepping out of a time machine. The point of the novel may be to teach readers that what they thought was temporally distant is morally contiguous, but that message begins in remoteness. This involves more than the span of years. Timothy Findley's *Famous Last Words* could have been subtitled " 'Tis Forty Years Since." Were its subject and setting Canadian, it would be discussed at length here. Nor is Hugh Hood's *The New Age* series, set in this country and at times in a more distant past than that of *Famous Last Words*, discussed in this work, because it deals with its time as a self-contained unit of the past, a time that has become archival. Hood's work emphasizes the flow of the past into present as, like all Romantic epics, it asserts the continuance of memory as the basis of consciousness. A more theoretical work, say one about time in the Canadian novel, could not ignore Hood's work, which involves a host of questions about the representation of time. That other critical book would also deal with science fiction, and the possibility of its role as a mirror-image to historical fiction. Such questions fall beyond this essay's scope.

A final note on that scope may seem less arbitrary than what has gone before. We have two official languages here. We may have two literatures. We may even have two literary cultures. Remote as the cultures may appear to one another, they share preoccupations common to national literatures. In both languages, the historical novel has served as a vehicle for the imaginative representation of nationalist ideologies. My discussion therefore treats the products of both cultures, though not comparatively. I do not discuss the unexpected parallels between literatures seemingly so diverse. I take it for granted that French and English Canada continue to occupy a single nation. They share similar concerns, though their hopes and fears take differing forms of expression. The danger of such a view is obvious, and I am not trying to work from a "One Canada" view of the country that irons out every significant regional and cultural difference. At the present time, that danger is slight. Our national culture, whatever that may be, seems in no great risk of losing its regional and diverse character. To put it more colloquially, if Quebec doesn't separate, then Alberta will. "Different" need not mean "alien"; "distinctiveness" need not imply "solitudinous." Including novels written in both official languages did not originate in my political views, though it certainly parallels them. The inclusion began, like this essay, in simple curiosity and observation, in readings convincing me that what I found in one langauge did not seem to involve a universe of discourse radically different from that found in another.

My aim throughout this essay has been one of discovering why those two strolling characters I mentioned at the beginning took along historical novels rather than Baedekers. This essay is a guidebook to the guidebooks.

NOTES

[1] See Gordon Roper, "New Forces, New Fiction 1880–1920," I, pp. 290–91; Desmond Pacey, "Fiction 1920–1940," II, pp. 172–73; and Hugo McPherson, "Fiction 1940–1960," II, p. 207 in Carl F. Klinck, ed., *The Literary History of*

Canada, 2nd. ed., 3 vols. (Toronto: Univ. of Toronto Press, 1976).

2 George Lukács, *The Historical Novel*, trans. Hannah and Stanley Mitchell (1938; London: Merlin, 1962); Ernest E. Leisy, *The American Historical Novel* (Norman: Univ. of Oklahoma Press, 1950); Robert A. Lively, *Fiction Fights the Civil War. An Unfinished Chapter in the Literary History of the American People* (Chapel Hill: Univ. of North Carolina Press, 1957); Lion Feuchtwanger, *The House of Desdemona: or, The Laurels and Limitations of Historical Fiction*, trans. and Foreword by Harold A. Basilius (Detroit: Wayne State Univ. Press, 1963); David Levin, *In Defense of Historical Literature. Essays on American History, Autobiography, Drama and Fiction* (New York: Hill and Wang, 1967); Jack Warwick, *The Long Journey; Literary Themes of French Canada* (Toronto: Univ. of Toronto Press, 1968); Michael Davitt Bell, *Hawthorne and the Historical Romance of New England* (Princeton: Princeton Univ. Press, 1971); Avrom Fleishman, *The English Historical Novel; Walter Scott to Virginia Woolf* (Baltimore: Johns Hopkins Univ. Press, 1971); James C. Simmons, *The Novelist as Historian; Essays on the Victorian Historical Novel* (The Hague: Mouton, 1973); Henderson, Harry B. III, *Versions of the Past: The Historical Imagination in American Fiction* (New York: Oxford Univ. Press, 1974); Andrew Sanders, *The Victorian Historical Novel, 1840–1880* (London: Macmillan, 1978); David D. Brown, *Walter Scott and the Historical Imagination* (London: Routledge and Kegan Paul, 1979); Mary Lascelles, *The Story-Teller Retrieves the Past: Historical Fiction and Fictitious History in the Art of Scott, Stevenson, Kipling, and Some Others* (Oxford: Clarendon, 1980); Donald S. Hair, *Domestic and Heroic in Tennyson's Poetry* (Toronto: Univ. of Toronto Press, 1981); Harry E. Shaw, *The Forms of Historical Fiction, Sir Walter Scott and His Successors* (Ithaca: Cornell Univ. Press, 1983).

3 Linda Hutcheon, "Canadian Historiographic Metafiction," *Essays on Canadian Writing*, No. 30 (Winter 1984–85), pp. 228–38. Sherrill E. Grace, "Structuring Violence: The Ethics of Linguistics in *The Temptations of Big Bear*," *Canadian Literature*, No. 104 (Spring 1985), pp. 7–22.

One

DURING THE NINETEENTH CENTURY, the Canadian historical novel was invariably a romance. A certain degree of surface realism may have obtained, especially in topographic and chronological detail. Yet no hero or heroine, even those few of lower-class origins, spoke in dialect or common speech. The chief impression left by the books is that of astonishing coincidences and dramatic encounters. Characters appear to have sprung from heroic molds. While the historical romance remains with us today, it no longer attracts writers of significance. That was not the case from 1832 (the date *Wacousta* appeared) to 1919 (a convenient date for marking the end of an era). Without exception, works written between 1832 and 1919 lean toward the romantic rather than the strictly novelistic in their structure and implication. While audiences then read fiction as they do today, unbothered by critical niceties as to the different kinds of fiction, this distinction is worth considering. To ponder it will strengthen the reader's sense of a shift in the techniques of literary presentation from era to era.

Frederic Jameson finds that the romantic hero is one who often remains submerged by a welter of narrative incident, a person trying to make sense of the mysteries surrounding him.

> Far from being an emissary of the "upper world", the hero of romance is something close to an observer, a mortal spectator surprised by supernatural conflict, who then himself is gradually drawn in to reap the rewards of victory without even quite being aware of what was at stake in the first place.[1]

Jameson suggests that the secularization of romance compels the writer to justify events according to the reality principle and to forsake the supernatural. The relevance of his remarks to the novels considered here becomes apparent.

We will encounter heroes thrown into a wilderness haunted

by ancestral feuds in which they become entangled (*Wacousta*); heroes trapped in the machinations of powerful figures (*The Golden Dog*); heroes victimized by conspiracies to deprive them of their birthright (*Une de perdue, deux de trouvées*); heroes whose ancestry and language compel them to renounce their dreams of love (*Les anciens Canadiens*) and heroes caught between warring empires whose struggles transform the heroes' lives (*The Seats of the Mighty*; *Jacques et Marie*). While the narratives focus upon heroic struggle and achievement, their conflicts arise from the clash of forces outside the hero. The heroes of these novels maintain an activist stance, but within a framework of passivity. Once in the arena, they fight; it is fate rather than an inbred pugnacity that lands them in the arena.

A characteristic of romantic narrative, as defined by Patricia Parker, employs a "strategy of deferral and dilation"[2] — the old soap-opera formula of "get the girl behind the eight-ball and keep her there." Repeatedly in these novels, the problems the hero faces frustrate and prolong his quest in a manner that recalls comedy no less than romance. Events conspire to part the lovers just when their union seems assured (and the novel shortened). Without exception, the novels feature complex plotting that produces delays. Lengthy flashbacks and abrupt shifts in narrative focus force the reader to await the resolution of a particular conflict. Suspense is an ancient narrative device, and the dilation it involves an abiding feature of these novels.

Other romantic motifs dot these novels. Northrop Frye has noted such recurring patterns as the loss or confusion of identity with a climax of self-recognition.[3] In these novels, that recognition can come about through solving the mysteries of one's parentage (*Une de perdue, deux de trouvées*), the revelation of an authentic, undisguised self (*Wacousta*) or the acceptance of a predetermined selfhood a character has tried in vain to escape (*Les anciens Canadiens*). Many of these novels deal with the descent into night worlds. The folk-tale devices of sorcery and enchantment yield to their rationalist counterparts of fevers, amnesias, imprisonments and the assumption of false identity, but the motifs remain.

Finally, Frye locates among all the marks of romantic narrative the common feature of the ultimately erotic nature of the romantic quest, the preoccupation with "the endless sexual stimulation of the wandering of desire."[4] In these novels, the male is the seeker. He duels with another male for the prize of his beloved (*The Seats of the Mighty*); offers violence to innocent parties when thwarted in love (*Wacousta*; *The Golden Dog*); fights against heavy odds to return to his distant beloved (*Jacques et Marie*); and risks his life to save his love's brother (*Les anciens Canadiens*).

Novels are more than collections of the common characteristics critics locate. For all formal kinship that stems from their romantic qualities, the novels here vary in many respects. In terms of the national mythologies they present, they align themselves around two poles. One group offers a national vision that is confident and inclusive, optimistic in its belief that the future holds for Canada the heap of prizes reserved for a unified and contented people. The other group defines its nationalism in terms of threat and exclusion. The future offers a continued struggle for survival. Unity becomes a necessity in the face of the enemy. The people must exclude those who threaten their solidarity. It might seem that the first ideology would originate in English Canada during its high imperial period, the second from French Canada. But that is not wholly correct. A perennial exception in almost any discussion of Canadian fiction confounds this neat polarity.

II

The French-Canadian novels in this chapter present a vision of nationalism whose emblem might be a closed fist rather than an open palm. They are joined by that strangest of English-Canadian fictions, John Richardson's *Wacousta*.[5]

Why do I discuss *Wacousta* in a treatment of historical fiction, especially of the sort dealing with nationalist themes? Is it not a lurid, Gothic adventure set in a wilderness stockade only because no castles loomed along the Detroit River in 1763? Since its chief formal source lies in the sentimental dramas of the eighteenth century, how can it be viewed as an example of historical fiction?[6] And how can *Wacousta* offer a glimpse into the nature of Canadian nationalism?

Wacousta's historical setting is more than a backdrop. The novel's events have their origin in two historical facts. Pontiac's uprising in 1763 is the proximate cause of what happens, but the defeat of the Scottish Jacobite rebels in 1715 is the first cause. Richardson's concept of history encases within a single continuum the two imperial incursions upon "backward" peoples and their doomed resistance. In brief, the novel tells the story of Reginald Morton, an English officer who loves a Jacobite girl, Clara Beverley. Morton's fellow officer, Charles De Haldimar, wins Clara through deception and frames Morton, who is court-martialled and disgraced. The novel opens decades later. Morton has become the dreaded Wacousta, Pontiac's evil genius, and De Haldimar is commander of Fort Detroit. Wacousta terrorizes the garrison and through a scheme of revenge destroys De Haldimar, his younger son Charles and his daughter Clara, before dying himself. The novel is told largely in flashbacks, and leaps from shocking,

3

suspenseful events to explanations of those events. Name changes, disguises and deceptions play a large role in the action; Reginald Morton's is not the only identity to be switched.[7]

What distinguishes this historical novel from so many others is its unique sense of Canadian history. Most of the other novels we will examine attempt to include the totality of the early Canadian experience. Their characters may be striving to subdue a raw wilderness or to strengthen a weak colonial society, but this reality belongs within a great and powerful empire that has already intruded upon the Canadian landscape. In a manner not to be encountered again until Philip Child's *The Village of Souls* (1933) and Louis Vaczek's *River and Empty Sea* (1950), Richardson uses that Old World reality only in flashbacks; it is present only as a backdrop to the disasters overtaking his characters, who are isolated in the Canadian wilderness. Our interest in him springs from his novel's encapsulation of the outlines of our contemporary anti-colonial ideology. Like Margaret Atwood's characters in *Surfacing*, Richardson's heroes are dropped into an alien Canadian wilderness without adequate resources. For example, in *Wacousta*, European military tactics are not suited to the frontier war that is being waged against the garrison. The resources of civilization seem remote and irrelevant. We are shown an unfriendly, limitless landscape: the garrison is on its own. At most, civilization can impose its own barbarities alongside those of the wilderness, as when De Haldimar has a nephew of Wacousta shot for a minor dereliction of duty. Compared with its nineteenth-century fellows, *Wacousta* could be seen as a psychohistorical novel. It delineates a reality in which history — in the sense of the recorded activities of the European empires — seems a remote process. A new history, a history of the outpost rather than of the settlement, is coming to be in the North American wilderness, but its stark polarities appear closer to the world of dream than to the modulated, dense textures of established colonial societies. On the one hand, in the novel, stands the garrison, with its rigid, vertical concept of order. On the other stretches the wilderness, its horizontality filled with terror. A bridge, on which much of the novel's significant actions occur, connects the two places. Wacousta's nephew is shot on the bridge, indicating that beneath the two opposed spaces lurks a connecting stratum, that of the shedding of innocent blood. Terror stalks both garrison and wilderness. The disguises indicate the deeper, unstable nature of the identity that the obsessive boundary-making seeks to buttress. The novel demonstrates the fragility of the barriers the penetrating European culture sets against the terror it thinks comes from the outside alone. The true history of the colonization of Canadian space becomes, in *Wacousta*, a primal encounter whose chief marks are fear and deception.

4

One of the first novels by a native-born Canadian, *Wacousta* offers little in the way of an overt nationalist ideology. Its author fought alongside Tecumseh in 1812 and was held in Kentucky as a prisoner of war. He subsequently sought a career in the British Army and returned to Canada after his irascible temperament closed off any future as a soldier. Yet his single memorable novel conveys the central problem of the fiction we are examining: what is the proper response to the fact of the Canadian forest landscape? *Wacousta* differs from its English-Canadian successors in its pessimism, its fear that a colonial remnant can be easily swallowed by an alien reality. That alien force exerts a pull over the garrison. It is, in fact, the product of forces the garrison has tried to disown, only to have them return in a more powerful guise. This pervasive sense of threat links *Wacousta* with the French-Canadian novels to be examined.

III

Threat limits choice. In the face of threat, alternatives are closed. Defensive postures demand rigidity, the exclusion of some courses of action in favour of others. What in happier situations could be boundaries to be explored become marches to be guarded. French Canada was once an outpost. Abandoned by its mother country, it fears absorption into the vast, undifferentiated mass of an English-speaking continent. Like the garrison in *Wacousta*, the society is on its own. Unless they are to be absorbed into the drives of the vast enterprise surrounding them, French Canadians must make final, determinative choices to set themselves firmly within the company of their own.

Philippe Aubert de Gaspé's *Les anciens Canadiens* (1863) seems in many ways a septuagenarian's pastoral on the *moeurs* of a bygone era. It nonetheless imposes an exclusionary choice as a means of cultural survival.[8] The novel's attraction lies in the twist love takes in the face of historical necessity. The climax of the novel occurs when, despite her love for him, Blanche d'Haberville refuses the hand of Archibald Cameron of Locheill. She will not dilute the blood-lines of French Canada. The harshness of her stance is emphasized by Locheill's origins. He is no typical *maudit anglais*: he is the son of a French mother and a Jacobite father who was killed at Culloden. He first encounters the seigneurial d'Haberville family in the person of Blanche's brother Jules, when they both attend a Quebec Jesuit college. There, as the novel opens in 1757, begins the historical process that will separate Locheill from Blanche. Despite Locheill's ancestry, the ties to Great Britain prove too strong to break. He

5

returns to Canada during the Seven Years' War as an officer in the British Army; Jules is fighting with the French. During the course of events, each man saves the other's life. Yet the imperial loyalties and structures keep them in adversarial roles. Though he attempts, at the war's end, to make amends, Locheill has followed Wolfe's orders during the contest and burned the d'Habervilles' farm. A less intently nationalist novelist would have used Locheill's remorse as a way of creating a variation on the Romeo–and–Juliet theme. After all, a French officer testifies that Locheill was reluctant to burn the farm, and Locheill spares no effort in his attempt to rehabilitate the d'Haberville fortunes. Jules marries an English girl; surely the gap is not too wide for the other lovers to cross? Yet Blanche refuses. Locheill passes his life in the service of others. Unlike other novels, especially those of English Canada, where romantic love bridges old hatreds, history and national necessity here divide the lovers.

The novel is chiefly thought of as a treasure house of bygone French-Canadian legends and customs, and the folkloric element threatens to overwhelm the slender plot. Many think its political themes can be ignored.[9] The novel describes rural festivals, feasts and maypole dances, and it presents the first literary treatment of the infamous local sorceress, La Corriveau. Fourteen years later, William Kirby includes her in *The Golden Dog*. In its text and in the notes the author appends, *Les anciens Canadiens* reconstructs a bygone era. A *nationaliste* critic has argued that the book is more than an exercise in nostalgia: it also presents a conservative tableau of a post-Conquest, Francophone elite as a model for the good society.[10] Is it fanciful to find Aubert de Gaspé's work the first imaginative instance of the anti-modernist, exclusionist Quebec nationalism that will persist for so long and flourish in the writings of the twentieth-century Abbé Lionel-Adolphe Groulx? Historical fiction need not always be conservative in its political implications; many novels examined later bear that out. Yet the genre seems generally conservationist in that it preserves in print the memory of bygone customs and habits. However politicized a reading one chooses to give *Les anciens Canadiens*, its conservationist excursions dovetail with Blanche's *grand refus*. Her decision not to marry is not to be taken as a retreat into sterility, but as an affirmation of a culture richly evoked and complete in itself. The one-time outpost has entrenched itself in the face of new threats and has developed its own memories and traditions. A patriarchal model of society can handle the threat of dilution when it comes from the female side, for Jules' English wife, like all good wives, will be absorbed into her husband's ways. The outsider male cannot be as easily accommodated. Hence Blanche's refusal, and the unwillingness of the novelist to permit romantic love to leap the barriers of history and culture.

6

The strength of those barriers asserts itself in the work of a lesser novelist, who uses a host of elevating devices to get his lovers over the walls. Ernest Choquette's *Les Ribaud* (1898) is set in 1837. Like many of the writers I will discuss, Choquette (1862–1941) shares nationalist concerns. He imposes a choice on his characters; it is less severe than the choice in Aubert de Gaspé's work, but a price is still exacted. Madeleine Ribaud weds Percival Smith, the English officer she loves. She is a model *patriote* who argues national questions with him at their first meeting. Despite his origins, Percival has a claim to Madeleine's attention. He has shown himself a man of feeling by weeping over the death of her hot-headed brother, who is killed in a duel with another English officer. The union of Madeleine and Percival is made palatable by the fact that Madeleine's father, Doctor Ribaud, is blood-thirsty and vengeful, and the *patriotes* are bombastic and self-seeking. By switching identities with another officer, Percival is saved from death in an ambush set by Doctor Ribaud; Madeleine takes her lover for dead until his reappearance. Doctor Ribaud, who "killed" Percival to preserve "l'orgeuil de mon nom, la dignité de ma race," comes to his senses when the noon-day gun (which stiffened him in bellicose pride) is followed by the ringing of the Angelus. The prayer restores him to a more humble Christian self.

In *Les Ribaud*, we have a man of feeling for a hero, an ogre for a father, clowns for rebels, death that comes as a result of mistaken identity, and a heroine who has a fainting fit. Only then can the Romeo–and–Juliet romantic attachment happen.

Les anciens Canadiens and *Les Ribaud* convey a motif in French-Canadian fiction that will carry over into the next century. The necessity to close ranks in the face of a perceived threat serves as a theme in French-Canadian historical fiction, and the theme of *la survivance* closely follows it. To close ranks is to produce the conditions for survival. Margaret Atwood's book *Survival* has shown how important the concept is in English-Canadian literature. In French Canada, survival has acquired a host of near-mythic associations. Yet as a leading French-Canadian historian pointed out, survival remains a passive concept. [11] Men and women of endurance and stoicism triumph through travail. One way to convey that triumph is to assert the moral superiority of the conquered to the victors. This is what happens in Napoléon Bourassa's *Jacques et Marie, souvenir d'un peuple dispersé* (1865). Father of nationalist editor Henri, Napoléon Bourassa (1827–1916) penned a *grande machine* of a historical romance. His book has both conservationist and nationalist aspects. His theme is the expulsion of the Acadians. The theme was first written about by Henry Wadsworth Longfellow in *Evangeline* (1847), one of the most popular poems of its day. Cultural nationalists may find it discomforting to realize that a United States historian, Francis Parkman, first exposed the romantic grandeur of France in North America to English-speaking readers. An American poet then produced the first imaginative treatment of the expulsion, which became a Canadian literary staple. In Bourassa's novel, the expulsion stands as a climactic moment in a process of moralized history through which the Canadiens demonstrate a clear moral superiority to their English overlords.

The Abbé Henri Raymond Casgrain made a critical pronouncement a year after Bourassa's novel appeared. Casgrain, Quebec's literary dictator, wrote that the time was ripe for the cultural flowering of French Canada. According to "Le mouvement littéraire au Canada," the struggle to establish the material foundations of civilized life was over. F. X. Garneau's *Histoire du Canada*, which appeared in 1845, gave writers a source-book on their nation's glorious past; *Les anciens Canadiens*, with its evocation of a storied past, appeared three years before the abbé's essay. The literary project could now go ahead, and Casgrain called for a literature that would be "largement découpée, comme nos vastes fleuves, nos larges horizons, notre grandiose nature, mystérieuse comme les échos de nos immenses et impénétrables forêts."[12] He also asked for autumn evenings, northern lights, deep blue skies and snowy winters. He then invoked his nation's history and demanded that its literature reflect that history. The meditative qualities of the missionary, the generosity of the martyr, the energy and perseverance of the pioneer, all must be part of that literary experience. His exaltation of passive heroism forced Casgrain to omit from his pantheon the figure of the soldier. This lapse complements the essay's general drift: Casgrain elevates the religious side of affairs and views the essential characteristics of the coming literature as "croyante et réligieuse." The society that literature would reflect was inconceivable without its beliefs: "sinon elle ne vivra pas, et se tuera elle-même." In a striking analogy, the critic declared that the French Canadians would serve as Mary to the Anglo-Saxon Martha, the Mary who had chosen the good part that shall not be taken away from her.[13]

The figure of speech could be seen as inexact; some nationalists would later find in their innocence a trap. But the conviction of moral superiority rests upon a scriptural source. There is Christianity's vision of triumphant humility; there is the preoccupation of the Romantic era with the picturesque and downtrodden. There is a powerful arsenal of images of exploitation, and of triumph in that exploitation. The victory of the humble is the theme of *Jacques et Marie*.

As Bourassa's title indicates, a love-interest shapes the novel; the reuniting of the lovers after their dispersion forms the story's central conflict. In their reunion will flourish the enduring qualities of the Acadians and, by extension, of all French Canadians. Stranded by history, abandoned by a careless mother country (the author mentions this on two occasions), the Acadians yet gain a moral victory. The novel begins in a golden, Arcadian age, in which all families share roughly the same amount of wealth and position, where marriages arise out of the simple fact of propinquity. Bourassa's moralized account ignores the complexity of the actual historical pressures involved; in his book, the English are the snake in the garden, though not in a simplistic way. [14]

Against the simple, straightforward wedding-cake lovers, the author has placed an English soldier, of the type we would now term a "white liberal." Bourassa compares his Acadians to the Trojan exiles of the *Aeneid* and likens their expulsion to Calvary; the language spoken by every evil-doer in the novel is English. Thus the reader expects to find an unqualified villain in the English soldier, Lieutenant George Gordon. He does press for Marie's hand during Jacques's lengthy exile, but that seems the extent of his voluntary transgressions. Like Locheill in *Les anciens Canadiens*, Gordon regrets the war crimes his side visits upon the Acadians. He spends as much time remonstrating with his own troops as he does fighting the nominal enemy. He seeks to shelter Marie and her family. Sympathetic but powerless, he receives, at the end of the novel, a Roman Catholic Baptism as he lays dying on the field at Ste. Foy. An endearing figure, he is helpless in the face of threatening forces. Success would have made him an unsuitable hero in this novel, where victories are moral. We see this when Marie's father, perhaps the most wronged man in the book, finds it in his heart to forgive the English even as Christ on the cross forgave the Jews. The author's exultation at the father's charity is not completely shared by the audience: scant pages before, the old man was vouchsafed a vision of the English commander in hell.

The net of forgiveness is not cast wide enough to include exogamy: Gordon must die in battle to ensure that Marie does not succumb to his attentions. With Gordon out of the way, Marie and Jacques can be reunited. The ending, a wedding surrounded by a host of folk rituals, reminds us that *la survivance* includes the retention of local custom.

We already witnessed an evocation of folk culture in *Les anciens Canadiens*, and we see a similar preoccupation in the work of Joseph Marmette (1844–95). Marmette was the first French-Canadian novelist to base his literary career on the writing of historical fiction, and his work proudly asserts its preservationist concerns. *Charles et Éva* (1886), *François de Bienville* (1870), *L'Intendant Bigot* (1872) and *Le Chevalier De Mornac* (1873) are poorly constructed melodramas interspersed with chunks of historical background, partly because Marmette was being didactic. He saw his function as similar to that of his father-in-law, the pioneering historian François-Xavier Garneau, whose heroic vision of Canadien history helped to shape a society's sense of itself.[15] Marmette's novels vary bizarre accounts of experience with pointed reminders to readers that this is all good for them.[16] Readers are faced with the sort of action and commentary that concludes *Bigot*: the villain, laden with ill-gotten gold, is caught in a shipwreck on his voyage back to France. Before his loot can pull him under, he is swallowed by a sea monster; "après le châtiment des hommes, était enfin venne la vengeance de Dieu."

Marmette's narratives are top-heavy with raw historical material. As well, there are discourses on customs, usages and topography. The crudely conceived heroes never flag in their devotion to New France. Their moral superiority to any enemy, whether English, traitorous French or Indian, is never in doubt. Marmette's novels may have earned their present obscurity, but they heighten the impression that French-Canadian historical fiction depicts New France as firm in its moral purity, exclusionist in its outlook and assured in its sense of moral election.

The themes and motifs we have been examining are also prominent in Georges Boucher de Boucherville's *Une de perdue, deux de trouvées*. Originally published as a monthly serial from 1849 to 1851 and then from 1864 to 1865, the work is a picaresque romance set in New Orleans and the Quebec of 1837. Impossible to summarize briefly, the plot concerns the efforts of Pierre St. Luc to extricate himself from the machinations of his Louisiana enemies and then to learn the secret of his parentage.

Something of a personal dilemma lurks behind the novel's events. Boucherville (1814–1894) was involved in the 1837 rebellion, was arrested and fled to the United States. In later years, he repudiated the cause of the rebellion.[17] The original version of the novel, published in 1849, contained no hint of Boucherville's rebel experiences, but in his revisions he proved more forthright about his original sympathies. In the novel, Pierre St. Luc is not forced to choose between the loyalist and rebel camps. The hero enjoys a freedom that the author, in retrospect, could well have wished for himself.

St. Luc arrives in Quebec to learn the secret of his birth just as the rebellion begins. He decides that, while *les fils de la liberté* (a group for whom Boucherville served as secretary, and whose manifesto he later repudiated) seemed like rebels, they were really seeking a redress of grievances. French Canadians remained loyal, as in 1812. Despite his sympathies, St. Luc chooses neither side; instead, he tries to learn about his ancestry. He later marries the daughter of an English general. His friend Calviera, who is really the Comte de Miolis, also marries an English girl. St. Luc is a free individual outside history; he can choose a partner without making a sacrifice. St. Luc's self-justifying magnetism sets him free, but the author uses a device to make his freedom possible.

French-Canadian historical fiction presents a nationalist vision based on fear and exclusion, a response to threats to survival. The threats are cultural and political, although authors locate them imaginatively in problems around mating. In English-Canadian fiction, the threat is posed by psychological predispositions that flourish in a lawless wilderness; in French-Canadian novels, the threat is posed by history.

The English-Canadian fiction examined in the rest of the chapter offers a contrasting view of nationhood. Its pervasive optimism discloses a culture (or a literary sideshow) buoyant in its assumptions of progress and the perpetuity of a social order.

IV

English-Canadian historical fiction at its high, romantic fullest, begins with William Kirby's *The Golden Dog* (1877) and Gilbert Parker's *The Seats of the Mighty* (1896).

In these two novels, individuals make history; decisive events are shaped by the energies of dynamic personalities. The love between man and woman is as important a force in the historical process as the strength of big battalions. The virtues that were successful then can win us victory now, because human dilemmas remain the same. Overtly or implicitly, these novels convey those ideas.

The Golden Dog and *The Seats of the Mighty* spring from an imperialist nationalism that once flourished in English Canada. A robust faith in "one Canada" displayed itself in dramas of conflict and resolution, where historical and cultural discontinuities are bridged. *The Golden Dog* works like a fable; *The Seats of the Mighty* is a swashbuckling adventure story. Both present to their readers the picture of a unified Canada that their sense of history confirms.

The Golden Dog offers an Upper-Canadian version of *Paradise Lost*, with a happy fall that produces a more enduring and legitimate order than one that could exist in an untouched Eden. [18] The novel opens in Eden, as a European visitor comments on the paradisal qualities he sees from aboard a ship in the St. Lawrence. Set in 1748 and based loosely upon an actual crime of the time, the story presents stark polarities that demonstrate that evil's triumph is only temporary. The dissolute seigneurial aristocrat, Le Gardeur de Repentigny, kills the honest *bourgeois*, Philibert, in a story that includes a moral anatomy of New France in its last days. New France falls through the accumulation of Old World corruption.

Kirby happened upon the basic outline of the story as it appeared in a series of antiquarian essays by a contemporary man of letters, Senator James M. Le Moine. From Le Moine's facts he assembled a series of moral tableaux, in which the divergencies between Old and New Worlds could take on parable-like dimensions. The chateau of a corrupt official, Bigot, resembles Versailles. Bigot schemes with the sexually compelling Angélique; the author twice hints that their plots are like those of Louis XV and Pompadour. Bigot's Parisian way of speaking contrasts with the speech patterns of the humbler *habitants*. His chateau brims with metropolitan luxury goods, the honest Philibert's with the staples of the country. Theological controversy over the rigorous Jansenist system of Roman Catholic devotional practice is viewed as an instance of Old World obsessions blighting the New.

The vanities and weaknesses of Le Gardeur, the aristocrat, snare him in the net of Bigot and Angélique. He cannot reside in the innocent shelter of his mother's manor house, and his restlessness throws him into a darker world. He is trapped in its toils and kills his beloved's father in a drunken rage, thus advancing Bigot's plots. The novel's events constitute a tragic pattern. The house of Philibert, in which the master fed twelve of the poor each day, has been eclipsed by Bigot's palace, in which an innocent New World girl is imprisoned. The colony is on the verge of dissolution.

Kirby could have ended the novel there, and no reader could have ignored the implication that New France's fall was occasioned more by moral than by material factors. The English-Canadian successor state established on the ruins of the colony would have been given a greater legitimacy, and the fall would have been for the best. Instead, Kirby attempted to come up with a myth of national commonality. The novel concludes with the reflection that, as New France became part of British North America, it entered into a bond with its English-Canadian counterpart. History merged the two Canadas into one as the virtue of loyalty became the trademark of both. English Canada had been founded, after the American Revolution, by United Empire Loyalists. Its origins and its spirited defense in 1812 indicated its sense of loyalty. How could French Canada be merged with English Canada? By its loyalty. It had demonstrated that loyalty to the Crown and its institutions in two ways. First, it had refused to desert its new masters during the American Revolution. Second, in 1813, it had resisted the American invasion at Chateauguay. To Kirby, the two Canadas proved to be one in their moral centre. The process of the fall of New France enhanced the society that was to occupy the top half of the continent.

Kirby's solution displays historical question-begging and distortion. But consider the knottiness of the problem he was trying to solve. How can one arrive at a sense of Canada that unites rather than divides its constituent parts? Assuming the nationalist enterprise to be worth it, where can one locate qualities that separate English Canada from the United States, yet link it with French Canada? Nearly twenty years after Kirby wrote *The Golden Dog*, Parker attempted a less moralistic version of reconciliation; he sought to locate the links within a myth of romantic love. The sexual magnetism that makes Angélique so meritricious in *The Golden Dog*, the sexual drives that threaten the purity of the cultural order in French-Canadian novels, the sexually motivated savageries that dot *Wacousta*: these energies are transformed, in *The Seats of the Mighty*, into forces that bring about an improved social order.

V

Parker's title, *The Seats of the Mighty*, recalls Kirby's pervasive moralism.[19] The title echoes the "Magnificat": "He hath put down the mighty from their seats, and exalted them of low degree" (Luke 1: 52). The author saw his story as an instance of the power of the humble to execute historic reversals. In the novel, an Anglo-American underdog plays a pivotal role in the founding of the New Canada. Sir Gilbert Parker (1862–1932) describes the aura of the little man; from the clash of rival empires comes a vindication of the powers of the individual, especially one seeking union with a beloved.

The question of choice that preoccupied Parker's near-contemporaries in French Canada expressed itself in the fact of sexual selection. In none of these works does the heroine exhibit any compelling sexual magnetism. Instead, the love-interest is wrapped up in the hero's quest for an ideal soulmate. This de-naturing of sexuality into clouds of romantic sentiment happens also in Parker's novel, but not to the extent that obtains elsewhere.

Parker grafted his love-interest on to the bare roots of historical fact. Historian Le Moine (the source of Kirby's novel) spotted the obscure *Memoirs* of Major Robert Stobo, who claimed an important role in the capture of Quebec.[20] Stobo's story, which Parker follows, tells of a captured Virginian officer of British birth in desperate circumstances. A prisoner on parole in Quebec, the officer had been caught spying and was returned to prison but engineered his escape. Parker's Robert Moray, like his actual counterpart, escapes from prison, then travels for thirty-eight days to meet General Wolfe. Moray shows Wolfe where to land the troops so they can ascend the heights. In his book, Stobo mentions a lady friend from the enemy camp who interceded with the Governor of Quebec on the officer's behalf. Parker bases the character of his heroine, Alixe, on Stobo's lady friend.

Parker gives Alixe the subservient role of the romantic heroine, but he also gives her other qualities. Elizabeth Waterston aptly sums them up: "Alixe is a real gem: a pure young girl who manages to dance like a courtesan, lie like a Machiavelli, dress first like a young officer then like a nun, slip undetected by sentries and even by her grim-faced father — and all in the name of virtue and constancy!"[21] The best example of this occurs when Alixe dances before a drunken crew at Bigot's palace — in the guise of a celebrated Parisian import — in order to distract the revellers from their plans for the imprisoned Moray. She dances before Moray as well, but the eroticism is purified by married love, since the dance follows their secret wedding.

The rivalry between Moray and Parker's villain, Doltaire, is sexual as well as political. They duel as soldiers and as opponents in a mating ritual. Moray, the hero, lacks the sexual aggressiveness of the villain. He clasps Alixe to his bosom from time to time, but his actions never have about them the whiff of hell-fire that marks Doltaire's attempt to seduce her. Doltaire's attempt seems perverse: it takes place within a convent while Moray watches from a secret alcove. What Waterston terms "Parker's . . . disturbing muffled erotic effects" are not always muffled.[22] Alixe tells Doltaire that "Disdainful nymphs are the better scabbard for distinguished swords" and it seems obvious that both parties know what they are talking about. As well, Moray displays a sado-masochistic streak in his account of a flogging that a reader may wish to view in the light of the novel's eroticism. The emotions Parker describes go beyond the ordinary boy–meets–girl story, and give the novel its special flavour.

Alixe remains pert but pure, but Moray's complexities provide a dark side to his conventional heroism. In describing Stobo's *Memoirs*, Le Moine admitted feeling uneasy about the ethical sleight-of-hand with which the soldier excused his spying while on parole.[23] Parker could have sanded away any flaws in his hero. Instead, he sticks to the record and Moray settles the question with an easy rationale: "When I found that they were determined and had ever determined to violate their articles, that they never intended to set me free, I felt absolved from my duty as an officer on parole, and I therefore secretly sent . . . a plan."

Moray is a man of action, someone who decides quickly and sleeps peacefully afterward. Alixe writes tender letters; Moray displays the toughness required of a leader. He is able to ignore the plight of others. We see this as he journeys to the English lines after his escape. He and his party stumble across two Indians who work for the French. The Indians are alarmed, and Moray's crew kill them. Moray comments laconically: "both lay there dead, two foes less of our King." He is also cool when he kills a jailer who had once befriended him. Both men are soldiers;

neither is squeamish about the fact that personal affection cannot always keep men on opposing sides from having to kill each other. Moray kills him and calls "that work . . . the worst I ever did in this world." Moray's brevity is typically English. The grief and guilt the speech indicates do not immobilize Moray; he remains calm.

His resilience lets him function with style and economy. His imprisonment and near-execution force him to undergo a number of symbolic deaths. He bounces back from each battle with renewed energy. "I had already suffered many deaths . . . and I would go to the final one looking like a man, and not like an outcast of humanity." He marshalls the requisite moral resources in challenging situations. Consider his final foray into Quebec. He stumbles over a dying French courier and steals his clothes, documents and horse. Riding in, Moray recalls that a uniformed courier needs a password. His realization is couched in noble words:

> Presently a thought pulled me up. The courier was insensible when I left him, and he was the only person who could help me in this. I reproached myself for leaving him while he was still alive. "Poor devil," thought I to myself, "there is someone whom his death will hurt. He must not die alone. He was no enemy of mine."

Moray finds out what he needs, then finds a safe house through the kindness of the soldier's widow.

Moray, a formidable figure, recalls one of John Buchan's gentleman spy-adventurers. Moray is not without feeling. He recites poetry to himself while in his cell; he frees a caged bird. He worships the woman he loves. Yet he is also an assured master of violence. Parker captures an imperial ideal in Moray, who strides through death and wreckage with righteous aplomb.

His certitude does not restrict itself to matters of personal safety. Moray comes to see the fall of New France as the last act of a morality play. He has a Victorian gift for the symbolic reading of an architectural vista. He first describes the set for the drama:

> In this space surrounding the Intendance was gathered the history of New France. This palace, large enough for the king of a European country with a population of a million, was the official residence of the commercial ruler of a province. It was the house of the miller, and across the way was the King's store-house La Friponne ["the scam": the name given to Bigot's corrupt circle], where poor folk were ground between the stone.

His description concludes with a detailed observation of the goods on display and the colourful crowd milling around them. The scene is marred by the marks of weakness Moray discerns:

> Behind a great collar of dogskin a pair of jet-black eyes flashed from under a pretty forehead; and presently one saw these same eyes grown sorrowful or dull under heavy knotted brows, which told of a life too vexed by care and labour to keep alive a spark of youth's romance.

It is an easy step to a moral theory about the fall of Quebec:

> I foresaw a strife, a complication of intrigues, and internal enmities which would be (as they were) the ruin of New France. I saw, in imagination, the English army at the gates of Quebec, and those who sat in the seats of the mighty . . . sacrificing the country; the scarlet body of British power moving down upon a dishonoured city, never to take its foot from that sword of France which fell there on the soil of the New World.

Moray's moralistic account of Quebec's fall resembles the stories that attracted Yankee Francis Parkman and Canadian Tory William Kirby. The fall of one regime engenders the redemption that will occur under English rule, where (presumably) the social injustice that blights the countenance of youth will be eradicated. Bishop John Strachan, who founded the college Parker attended and later taught in, had put forward a providential theory of the establishment of Upper Canada.[24] Strachan said that the expulsion of the Loyalists from the thirteen colonies brought about a new and better society.[25] Parker's variation on this theme ignored such material agents for the fall as over-extended supply lines and underpopulation, and fulfills a political as well as a literary aim. Politically, it justifies the English-dominated political order that followed New France. As well, it dovetails with the inescapable idealism of romantic narrative. Moray expresses his love for Alixe in terms of a heroic individualism that transcends all moral bounds: "there comes a time when a man has a right to set all else aside but his own personal love and welfare, and to me the world was now bounded by just so much space as my dear Alixe might move in." The energy that sprang from their love enabled the couple to shape history as well as their personal destinies. Moray showed Wolfe the footpath because he wanted to rescue Alixe from her confinement in Quebec and because he wanted to win the war. Romantic love (and the bourgeois domestication of it, ideal marriage) carries before it both personal and national fates.

Alixe needed a compelling sexuality and Moray a smoothly functioning will–to–power so they would be more than an interesting fillip to the conventions of popular romance. In winning Alixe, Moray wins a French Canada distinguished by a natural *joie de vivre* yet which never fails to know its place in the power structure. The English gain "the rare and winning earth" that Moray beheld from the heights of Quebec. The couple's union "had been a national matter — of race and religion." This *union nationale* ties French imaginativeness, style and ingenuity to English efficiency, boldness and resolution. The successor state to the old regime was not imposed: it married its predecessor. In Parker's novel, a smooth, uninterrupted flow characterizes Canadian history. A providential fall brought about the union of the best of two races. Sexuality is harnessed to power the political order. The fear and exclusivity that stands out in many other historical novels yields to a serene confidence that the social order can accommodate all human drives.

At a time when political, social, and cultural habits were going through radical shifts, when individuals seemed powerless to stem the flow of collective currents, historical novels such as *The Seats of the Mighty* gave the pleasure, to a large audience, of hearing an old story retold.[26] New versions of the same tale assert that human nature remains essentially the same, and that the devices for coping with perennial problems also remain the same. True love, a stout heart and a bit of luck will triumph in the end.

Yet the discontinuous origins of the Canadian state keep intruding. How does one arrive at a sense of "one Canada" and still acknowledge its origins in fracture and defeat? A nationalist French-Canadian writer takes as a starting point a view of the *Canadien* nation as an organism trapped within a larger, alien organism that threatens it; exclusionary choices must be made to preserve the *Canadien* integrity. Outsiders are incorporated only after they have passed various trials or under special circumstances. English-Canadian writers, on the other hand, must invoke a version of history that has been moralized or mediated by erotic conquest. The English-Canadian writers erected a historical framework around the two societies that sheltered both.

This is apparent in the work of two writers, John L'Esperance (1838–1891) and Wilfred Campbell (1858–1918). L'Esperance's *The Bastonnais, A Tale of the American Invasion of Canada in 1775–6* (1877) and Campbell's *A Beautiful Rebel: A Romance of Upper Canada in Eighteen Hundred and Twelve* (1909) deal with two lovers in a time of war. In both books, the lovers discover that the wickedness of their mate is not as apparent by the end as it was in the beginning. The lovers reach a compromise; the once-warring parties unite in a commitment to Canada's destiny. *The Seats of the Mighty* follows the same themes on a larger scale.

Parker and Kirby both present a picture of New France as English

Canada's mythical second self. In the nineteenth century, Canada was trapped in modernity. The country viewed itself as different from the United States. The "one Canada" would come from English Canada, with its Loyalist roots, an imperial solution to an American disturbance, and from French Canada, a more organic and picturesque entity than any the United States could furnish. A society marked by heroic individualism, swayed by personal passions that advanced a political project: this was the dream of romantic Canada. Kirby and Parker imaginatively annealed the two Canadas into a single, continuous process of North American occupation. On the one hand, a developing technological culture; on the other, a storied past. According to their synthesis, no longer would the reality and the dream war within the bosom of the Canadian state. In fact, the synthesis would always be open to challenge. In his satire, *Sunshine Sketches of a Little Town*, Stephen Leacock questioned the idealized version of Canadian history.

Aboard the *Mariposa Belle*, two of the town's citizens cross-talk about the systems of belief that give coherence to the world. During the marine excursion of the Knights of Pythias, Dean Drone discerns traces of the hand of God in the landscape. Doctor Gallagher, on the other hand, spots only evidences of Champlain's explorations. The scientific historiography of the nineteenth century had validated Doctor Gallagher's vision of secular history. Historical novelists gave imaginative scope and resonance to that secular explanation of Canada's roots and destiny.

The two nationalisms glimpsed in this chapter's subjects provided alternative views of Canadian reality. One saw that reality in terms of a besieged fortress that protected a garden. Behind that fortress, the garden could flourish. The customs and liturgies of the people became the content of the novels (the garden), while the necessity for choice served as their theme (the fortress). The other nationalism also saw a garden, but one that needed no fortress as protection, because the garden possessed the assimilative powers of a jungle. Through assimilation and annexation, new growths could be absorbed into the hybrids to which the plantation was constantly giving birth.

The period covered in the next chapter was to witness a shift in both nationalisms. The first would discover a sense of tragedy and the dispersion of energy in the materials it had traditionally worked with. The second would find its confidence sapped and a dimension of terror added to its material. The second nationalism returned to the fevered wilderness *Wacousta* had explored. What seemed a sport would prove, like many a mutation, to be a hardy genetic source.

1 Frederic Jameson, "Magical Narratives: Romance as Genre," *New Literary History*, 7 (Autumn 1975), 139, 145.

2 Patricia Parker, *Inescapable Romance. Studies in the Poetics of a Mode* (Princeton: Princeton Univ. Press, 1979), p. 182.

3 Northrop Frye, *The Secular Scripture, A Study in the Structure of Romance* (Cambridge: Harvard Univ. Press, 1976), pp. 54, 104, 145, 152.

4 Frye, p. 30.

5 To avoid extensive notes, I have not given the specific location of brief passages from the novels discussed here. I do list the usual information on publication in the bibliographies provided for each chapter.

6 For the novel's debt to eighteenth-century drama, see Sandra Djwa in "Letters in Canada 1976," *University of Toronto Quarterly*, 46, No. 4 (Summer 1977), 473–74.

7 Treatments of *Wacousta* can be found in Michael Hurley, "*Wacousta*: The Borders of Nightmare," in John Moss, ed., *The Canadian Novel*, vol. II of *Beginnings. A Critical Anthology* (Toronto: NC, 1980), pp. 60–69; Robert Lecker, "Patterns of Deception in *Wacousta*," *Journal of Canadian Fiction*, No. 19 (1977), pp. 77–85; Robin Mathews, "John Richardson: The Wacousta Factor," in *Canadian Literature: Surrender or Revolution*, ed. Gail Dexter (Toronto: Steel Rail, 1978), pp. 13–25; John Moss, *Patterns of Isolation in English Canadian Fiction* (Toronto: McClelland and Stewart, 1974), *passim*, and *Sex and Violence in the Canadian Novel: The Ancestral Present* (Toronto: McClelland and Stewart, 1977), pp. 84–90; Margot Northey, *The Haunted Wilderness: The Gothic and Grotesque in Canadian Fiction* (Toronto: Univ. of Toronto Press, 1976), pp. 18–26; my "John Richardson," in *Canadian Writers and Their Works*, Fiction Series, Vol. I, eds. Robert Lecker, Jack David, and Ellen Quigley (Toronto: ECW, 1983), pp. 117–31, and *Gardens, Covenants, Exiles: Loyalism in the Literature of Upper Canada/Ontario* (Toronto: Univ. of Toronto Press, 1982), pp. 46–53.

8 I owe a debt that borders on plagiarism to a number of studies of French–Canadian historical fiction. In order of usefulness, they are: Maurice Lemire, *Les Grands Themes nationalistes du roman historique canadien-français* (Québec: l'Université Laval, 1970); David M. Hayne, *The Historical Novel and French Canada* (Diss. Ottawa 1945); Madeleine Ducrocq-Poirier, *Le Roman Canadien de langue française de 1860 à 1958. Recherche d'un esprit romanesque* (Paris: A. G. Nizet, 1978); Roger Lemoine, "Le roman historique au Canada français," *Archives des lettres canadiennes*, E. III (1964), pp. 69–87, and another article of the same title in his *Le roman Canadien français* (Ottawa: Fides, 1964), pp. 69–87.

In a class by itself, and of immense help to any student of the literature of French Canada, stands the encyclopaedic *Dictionnaire des oeuvres littéraires du Quebec*. Tome I, des origines a 1900; Tome II, 1900–1939 (Montréal: Fides,

1978–80). Edited by Maurice Lemire, the volumes contain brief summaries, evaluations and biographical entries that cover the whole of *Canadien* belles-lettres. I have relied on these volumes heavily.

9 As an example of this, see J. S. Tassie, "Philippe Aubert de Gaspe," in *Our Living Tradition*, second and third series, ed. Robert L. McDougall (Toronto: Univ. of Toronto Press, 1959), pp. 55–72. For an astute assessment of the novel's politics, see Ben Shek, "In the Beginning Was the Conquest," in Norman Penner, ed., *Keeping Canada Together Means Changing Our Thinking* (Toronto: Amethyst, 1978), pp. 12–24.

10 Nicole Deschamps, "Les 'anciens Canadiens' de 1860: une societe de seigneurs et va-nu-pieds," *Études francaises*, 1 (Oct. 1965), 3–15. See also Enn Raudsepp, "Patriotism and Class Interest in *Les anciens Canadiens*," *Journal of Canadian Fiction*, No. 30 (1980), pp. 106–13.

11 "As a collectivity, the *Canadiens* were doomed to an anemic survival. One must never forget that to survive is not to live. However, the *Canadiens* consoled themselves in believing their survival a miracle . . . . The fact is that *Canadiens* had no choice but to survive." Michel Brunet, "French Canadian Interpretations of Canadian History," *The Canadian Forum*, April 1964, p. 7.

12 Examples of this abound in Carl Berger, *The Sense of Power* (Toronto: Univ. of Toronto Press, 1970), pp. 128–33.

13 Casgrain's essay: *Oeuvres Complètes*, T. 1 (Montréal: Beauchemin, 1896), pp. 353–75. See esp. pp. 368–71.

14 One can hold that while the Acadians scarcely deserved what happened to them at the hands of the English, the whole sorry business grew out of causes other than British greed and callousness. English-Canadian historical novelists spend some time exonerating British authorities from blame, but those same writers also tend to present a more complex sense of the forces involved than do their French-Canadian counterparts. See my "Nouvelle(s) France: An Impression," *Queen's Quarterly*, 88 (Spring 1981), 50–51.

15 François-Xavier Garneau, *Histoire du Canada*, 6th édition, 2 tomes (Paris: Librairie Alcan, 1920 [1845–69]); English edition: *History of Canada*, trans. Andrew Bell, two volumes (Montreal: Lovell, 1862).

   For information on Marmette's life and career, see Roger Le Moine, *Joseph Marmette, sa vie, son oeuvre, suivi de à Travers La Vie, roman de mouers Canadiennes* (Québec: Univ. Laval, 1968).

16 "Il en est tant de Canadiens, dans nôtre pays, qui oublient ce qu'ils sont ou ce qu'ils auraient dû être, qu'il faut bien que quelqu'un leur rapelle de temps à autre, et leur redise ce qu'ils semblant méconnaître ou avoir oublié, à savoir que nous n'avons pas a rougir de nôtre arbre genealogique, et que nous devons conserver, *sans honté*, la langue et les usages de nos peres." (emphasis in original) *Charles et Eva*, pp. 173-74.

   "Mon devoir est de rendre populaires, en les dramatisant, des actions nobles et glorieux qui tout canadien devrait connaître." *François de Bienville*, p. 9.

[17] For information on Boucherville, see Reginald Hamel's "Présentation" to *Une de perdue, deux de trouvées* (Montréal: Hurtubise, 1973); see also Maurice Lemire's entry on the novel in his *Dictionnaire*, I, pp. 720–28.

[18] My *Gardens, Exiles, Covenants* contains a closer examination of the novel, from which these statements about it derive.

[19] See L. R. Early, "Myth and Prejudice in Kirby, Richardson, and Parker," *Canadian Literature*, No. 81 (Summer 1979), pp. 24–36.

[20] J. M. Le Moine, "Major Robert Stobo," in his *Maple Leaves*, 4th series (Québec: Augustin Coté, 1873), pp. 55–73; [Robert Stobo], *Memoirs of Major Robert Stobo of the Virginia Regiment* (Pittsburgh: John S. Davidson, 1854).

[21] Elizabeth Waterston, "Introduction" to Sir Gilbert Parker, *The Seats of the Mighty* (Toronto: McClelland and Stewart, 1971), p. vii.

[22] Waterston, p. vii.

[23] Le Moine, pp. 57–58.

[24] For information on Parker's career, see John Coldwell Adams, *Seated with the Mighty* (Ottawa: Borealis, 1979).

[25] For information on Strachan, see S. F. Wise, "Sermon Literature and Canadian Intellectual History," United Church Committee on Archives, *The Bulletin* (1965), pp. 13–15.

[26] "The year 1896 was marked by the widespread reading of Frederic J. Stinson's *King Noanett*, a story of seventeenth-century England and America, and Sir Gilbert Parker's *The Seats of the Mighty*, about Wolfe's capture of Quebec." James D. Hart, *The Popular Book, a History of America's Literary Taste* (New York: Oxford Univ. Press, 1950), p. 203.

BIBLIOGRAPHY*

Adam, G. Mercer, and A. Ethelwyn Wetherald. *An Algonquin Maiden: A Romance of the Early Days of Upper Canada*. Montréal: John Lovell, 1887 [available in Toronto Reprint Library of Canadian Prose and Poetry, 1973].

Boucherville, Georges Boucher de. *Une de perdue, deux de trouvées*. Edition présentée par Reginald Hamel. Montréal: Hurtubise, 1973.

Bourassa, Napoléon. *Jacques et Marie: Souvenir d'un peuple dispersé*. Texte Établi et Presenté par Roger LeMoine. Montréal: Fides, 1976.

Burnham, Hampden. *Marcelle: An Historical Novel*. Toronto: William Briggs, 1905.

Campbell, Wilfred. *A Beautiful Rebel: A Romance of Canada in Eighteen–hundred and twelve*. Toronto: Westminster, [1909].

---

*I have given dates of original publication when they disagree with those of the edition I have used, except for works whose original date I have included in the text.

Included also is information on English translations of works in French, since I have used them as trots.

Chauveau, P.J.O. *Charles Guerin: roman de moeurs Canadiennes.* Edition presentée et annotée par Maurice Lemire. Montréal: Fides, 1978 [1846–53].

Choquette, Ernest. *Les Ribaud: Une idylle de 37.* Montréal: Sénécal, 1898.

Collins, Edmund. *Annette. The Metis Spy; A Heroine of the N. W. Rebellion.* Toronto: Rose Publishing Co., 1886.

Crawley, Mary Catherine. *A Daughter of New France.* Toronto: Musson, 1901.

De Gaspé, Philippe Aubert. *Les anciens Canadiens.* Montréal: Fides, n.d. Translated into English by Sir Charles G. D.Roberts as *Canadians of Old.* Toronto: McClelland and Stewart, [1890].

De Mille, James. *The Lily and the Cross: A Tale of Acadia.* Boston and New York: Lee and Shepard, 1875.

Hart, P.W.E. *Jason — Nova Scotia.* New York: Bibelot Bros., 1903.

Heavysege, Charles. *The Advocate.* Montreal: Richard Worthington, 1865 [available in Toronto reprint Library of Canadian Prose and Poetry, 1973].

Hickey, David. *William and Mary. A Tale of the Siege of Louisburg, 1745.* Toronto: Wm. Briggs, 1884.

John, Alix [Alice Jones]. *The Night Hawk. A Romance of the '60s.* Toronto: Copp, Clark, 1901.

Kirby, William. *The Golden Dog (Le Chien D'Or), a Romance of Old Quebec.* Toronto: Musson, [1925]. A New Canadian Library edition is also available. All but the very first edition — *Le chien d'or, the golden dog, a legend of Quebec* (New York and Montreal: Lovell, Adam, Wesson, 1877) — have been abridged by one hand or another.

Laut, Agnes C. *Heralds of Empire, Being the Story of One Ramsay Stanhope, Lieutenant to Pierre Radisson in the Northern Fur Trade.* Toronto: William Briggs, 1902.

———. *Lords of the North.* Toronto: William Briggs, 1900.

Leprohon, Roseanna. *Antoinette de Mirecourt or, Secret Marrying and Secret Sorrowing.* Introduction by Carl Klinck. Toronto: McClelland and Stewart, 1973 [1864].

L'Esperance, John. *The Bastonnais. Tale of the American Invasion of Canada in 1775–6.* Toronto: Belford, 1877.

Lighthall, William Douw. *The False Chevalier or the Lifeguard of Marie Antoinette.* Montreal: Grafton, 1898.

Macdonnell, Blanche Lucile. *Diane of Ville Marie. A Romance of French Canada.* Toronto: William Briggs, 1898.

[A.M.M.] Machar, Agnes Maule. *For King and Country: A Story of 1812.* Toronto: Adam, Stevenson & Co., 1874.

MacKie, John. *The Rising of the Red Man: A Romance of the Louis Riel Rebellion.* London: Jarrold & Sons, 1902.

Marmette, Joseph. *Charles et Éva.* Montréal: Éditions Lumen, 1945.

———. *Le Chevalier de Mornac: Chronique de la Nouvelle- France 1664.* Montréal: Hurtubise, 1972.

———. *Francois de Bienville. Scenes de la vie Canadienne a XVIIe siecle*. Québec: Léger Brousseau, 1870.

———. *L'Intendant Bigot*. Montréal: Desbarats, 1872.

Marquis, T.G. *Marguerite de Roberval: A Romance of the Days of Jacques Cartier*. Toronto: Copp, Clark, 1899.

McIlwraith, Jean N. *A Diana of Quebec*. Toronto: Bell & Cockburn, 1912.

———. *The Curious Career of Roderick Campbell*. Toronto: Macmillan, 1901.

McLennan, William. *In Old France and New*. New York: Harper, 1899.

——— . and Jean N. McIlwraith. *The Span O' Life. A Tale of Louisbourg and Quebec*. New York: Harper, 1899.

McLeod, A.J. *The Notary of Grand Pré. A Historic Tale of Acadia*. Boston: Published by the author, 1901.

McPhail, Sir Andrew. *The Vine of Sibmah. A Relation of the Puritans*. New York: Macmillan, 1901.

Parker, Sir Gilbert. *The Power and the Glory: A Romance of the Great La Salle*. New York: Harper, 1925.

———. *The Seats of the Mighty, Being the Memoirs of Captain Robert Moray, Sometime an Officer in the Virginia Regiment and after of Amherst's Regiment*. Vol. IX of the Imperial Edition of his Works. New York: Scribner's, 1916. (The 1971 New Canadian Library Edition, containing Elizabeth Waterston's valuable Introduction, is abridged.)

———. *The Trail of the Sword*. Toronto: Copp, Clark, 1898 [1894].

Richardson, John. *Wacousta: A Tale of the Pontiac Conspiracy*. Toronto: Historical Publishing Co., 1906. Every edition of the novel except the first — *Wacousta; or, the Prophecy*, 3 vols., London: T. Cadell, 1832 — has been abridged, though none to the extent of the 1967 New Canadian Library Edition.

Rousseau, Edmond. *La Monongahéla*. Québec: Darveau, 1890.

Roberts, Sir Charles G. D. *The Forge in the Forest: Being, the Narrative of the Acadian Ranger*, etc. New York: Grosset & Dunlap, 1896.

———. *The Prisoner of Mademoiselle*. Toronto: Copp, Clark, 1904.

———. *The Raid from Beauséjour and How the Carter Boys Lifted The Mortgage. Two Stories of Acadie*. Toronto: Musson, [1894].

———. *A Sister to Evangeline, Being the Story of Yvonne de Lamourie*, etc. Boston: Lanson Wolffe & Co., 1898.

"Malcolm" [Coll MacLean Sinclair]. *The Dear Old Farm. A Canadian Story*. St. Thomas, Ont.: The Journal, 1897.

Sladen, Douglas. *Lester the Loyalist. A Romance of the Founding of Canada*. Tokio: the Hakubunsha, 1890.

[Tenney, Rev. E. P.] *Constance of Acadia: A Novel*. Boston: Roberts Brothers, 1886.

Withrow, William. *Barbara Heck, A Tale of Early Methodism*. Toronto: William Briggs, [1895].

———. *Neville Trueman, The Pioneer Preacher: A Tale of the War of 1812*. Toronto: William Briggs, 1900.

Two

"Although the historians of political nationhood wrote large tomes full of political and constitutional acts and facts, their national consciousness was basically romantic and idealist."[1]

WHAT BETTER SPUR FOR THE WRITING OF HISTORICAL fiction than a romantic and idealist consciousness? Our examination of the novels of the first chapter indicated how firmly that romantic, idealist tradition governed the books written in the nineteenth century. The books examined in this chapter demonstrate the endurance of that spirit and indicate some modifications of it as well: realism begins to play a greater role in the conventions that shape the narratives.

From about 1900 to 1970, the Canadian historical novel moved from romantic idealism to a less gaudy realism. The finest works range from Philip Child's *The Village of Souls*, a visionary account of initiation into the Canadian reality, to Louis Vaczek's realistic treatment of the same theme, *River and Empty Sea*. Among the interesting French-Canadian works of this time are those of Léo-Paul Desrosiers.

Nationalistic themes are also treated differently. Before 1900, the novel promoted some form of the Canadian state, whether a post-Confederation, English-dominated state or the *nation* of French Canada. After 1900, though, novels began to embrace something at once more and less than a political entity: the new allegiance was to an environment, the wilderness environment of the New World.

The theme of choice remained significant, but it was no longer marked by an exclusivity. In some novels, a Continentalist, English-dominated entity was affirmed; others expressed a commitment to the survival of a French-speaking entity. Both themes excluded the Old World, and did not seek to differentiate between portions of the new. There is little sense of two nationalisms warring within the bosom of a single literature.

24

These statements are subject to qualification. Novels involving derring-do, bizarre coincidence and heroic characters continued to appear; even today, a fossilized form of historical fiction is being written. But this essay will deal with developments in the genre, and with the books that helped to change the genre.

My interest in development accounts for the length of the period discussed in this chapter. The Canadian historical novel began to flower with the appearance, in 1970, of Anne Hébert's *Kamouraska*; no romance with the verve of Parker's *The Seats of the Mighty* appeared after 1896. Most novels written between 1900 and 1970 repeated familiar formulas; only a few novels took the form in new directions. This chapter focusses on continuity and change, on books that helped to reshape the practices and themes contained in novels written before 1900. A near-mystical sense of allegiance to the new land marks the novels written after 1900. Allegiance to the new environment encloses and justifies the choices made by the characters in these novels.

The next three sections of this chapter treat the material in a non-chronological fashion; the novels are linked by thematic and structural similarities. As one novelist of the time indicated, historical fiction can be seen as a kind of science-fiction in reverse: the books deal with an area of experience that is walled off by past time rather than by future time.[2] I have arranged my subjects by theme rather than by date of appearance.

The chapter discusses three themes: choice, the preservation of society against hostile forces and the image of national reconciliation. As well, we examine these themes in novels where they are expressed in a darker manner, where they point to unresolved conflicts. Finally, there is a discussion of two Canadian novels of finer quality than others in the chapter. They differ in technique and in message. Both demonstrate developments that occurred in the genre between 1900 and 1970.

II

In historical fiction, choice and an affirmation of the new land often proceed together. They do in the fiction of "Laure Conan," the pseudonym of Félicité Angers (1845–1924).[3] Quebec's first woman novelist, Conan is remembered chiefly for her psychological novel, *Angéline de Montbrun* (1884). Conan also wrote three historical novels, which send forth the traditional, clerical nationalist message that Quebec is God's beach-head in the New World. Like some later novels, Conan's books rely upon the depiction of intense psychological and emotional states.

Her best, *La sève immortelle* (1925), was written when the author was on her deathbed and published posthumously. It is similar in theme to Aubert de Gaspé's *Les anciens Canadiens*. The difference, significant in view of the exclusionist nationalism we met earlier, lies in the fact that Conan presents a choice between Canada and France, rather than between French and English Canada. The choice is embodied in two contrasting heroines. Conan's hero, Jean Le Gardeur de Tilly, also emphasizes the book's nineteenth-century ties: he is similar to the protagonist in *The Golden Dog*.

The devices used by historical novelists to present the theme of choice are limited. We encountered symbolic death in *Les Ribaud* and in *The Seats of the Mighty*; we shall meet it again in *Hangman's Beach*. *La sève immortelle* opens with a symbolic death: a nun nurses the near-mortal wounds our hero received at Ste. Foy. In the familiar nationalist trope of New France's betrayal by the mother country, the nun declares that France's abandonment of its offspring will not prevent New France from remaining true to itself. Two chapters later, Tilly will dream of a Canada still wrapped in the French flag. Before such a renewal can happen, choices must be made. Guillemette, a Canadian-born woman, must refuse the hand of Lieutenant Laycraft (a decent *anglais* of the type encountered in *Les anciens Canadiens*), even though her father has approved the match. Tilly must see his love, Thérèse, and her family return to France. Though he terms his fellow colonials "les naufragés," he refuses to leave the scene of the disaster. After her ship sails, Thérèse dies of pneumonia; Tilly secures Guillemette's hand and declares his faith in the land: "La terre n'a jamais laissé mourir de faim ceux qui l'aiment."

The benefits of choosing correctly are clear: Tilly lives and Thérèse dies. The title indicates that Tilly's role as the vigour of the new society extends beyond making a "grand refus" of Old France; he must align himself positively in the new. In one of Conan's earlier novels, *A l'oeuvre et à l'épreuve* (1891), there was a renunciation of love for sacred reasons as the hero wended his way toward martyrdom in the Jesuit missions. But *La sève immortelle* bestows on the secular mandate of romantic nationalism the power to impose a vocation superior to that of romantic love. In *The Seats of the Mighty*, sexual bonding contains a force compatible with the fulfillment of a national vision. In *La sève immortelle*, the sentimental plot line does not work as such devices often work; the individual fulfillment promised by romantic attachment must give way to the collective goals of nationalism.

Conan's *L'oublié* (1900) appeared between *A l'oeuvre et à l'épreuve* and *La sève immortelle*. *L'oublié* denotes the secularization that overtook Conan, generally a pietistic novelist. It is an account of the era of Montreal's first governor, Maisonneuve ("the forgotten" of the title), and its nationalism is couched in the imagery of Scripture:

C'est une colonie d'apôtres, de héros, qui semble une seule famille
. . . . Ils vivent commes les fidèles de la primitive Église vivaient,
en attendant l'heure du martyre.

The novel describes the love of Lambert Closse for Elisabeth Moyen, whom
he marries. His devotion to his wife does not prevent him from springing
to the colony's defense when Maisonneuve calls, and Closse dies fighting
the Iroquois at the legendary Long Sault. At the end of the novel, Maisonneuve delivers Closse's musket to Elisabeth's door.

The blood of martyrs is the seed of the Church. Spiritual and secular
themes converge in L'oublié, and the forgotten ones struggle in a sacred
national cause. By 1925, when La sève immortelle is published, this cause
stands on its own. Conan's three historical novels preach renunciation. Yet
in La sève immortelle, blame for the heroine's death is placed on the
shoulders of those faithless to New France. Thus the pattern of martyrdom can be modified. An other-worldly ethos becomes a secular ethos.
La sève immortelle indicates the tenacity of the clerical version of Quebec
nationalism; it also shows the cracks that appeared in the monolith as the
secular impulse began to supplant the sacred one.

In Conan's fiction, the theme of choice involves an affirmation of the
new land. As she moved from a pietistic national vision to a secular one,
Conan revealed an inner development uncommon in writers who discuss
this theme, and who take for granted the idea of secular fulfillment as part
of the nationalist surge. Such novels begin where Conan left off, but the
writers never extend themselves as Conan was able to do. In two novels,
Quietly My Captain Waits (1940) and Restless Are the Sails (1941), Evelyn
Eaton (1902–) offers the familiar love plots of popular romance; her lovers
always choose to cling to the freedoms of the New World. Her theme ex-
ercised a special appeal during World War Two. The theme also persists
in other works, written at other times. It flourishes, for example, in the
little-known The Forging of the Pikes (1920) by "Anison North" (May
Wilson). North uses a strange blend of Upper Canadian radicalism and
primitivism to justify the 1837 uprising; her lovers paddle off into the sunset
to escape the excesses of civilization. A justly forgotten work, A. Ermatinger
Fraser's The Drum of Lanoraye (1932), uses the motif of Old World corruption versus New World innocence to praise the "simpler, happier life
in a new land" and Canada in the present. In the melodramatic Three Came
to Ville Marie, writer Alan Sullivan concluded the story with the characters'
decision to remain on this side of the water. The same theme appears in
works that are not melodramatic; for example, Ethel Mary Granger Bennett's solidly constructed novels: Land for Their Inheritance (1955), A Straw
in the Wind (1958) and Short of the Glory (1960). The three books offer

convincing accounts of the lives led by the inhabitants of New France. Yet in her attempt to account for the significance of this often harsh experience, Bennett relies on affirmation and assimilation as reasons. In the second novel, Acadians evolve into Nova Scotians. In the third, in a vision, the wars between England and France cease and the Acadians agree "to exist peacefully together on the North American continent, respecting each other's differences and even . . . enjoying them."

"Immigrant" assimilationist fiction is important in United States literature, yet appears to be absent from ours. But ours has been written in a different way. We have chosen to locate our New Canadians in almost any time but the present. For every novel like *The Sacrifice* (1956), there are half a dozen that set the conflict between the culture of the old and the promise of the new in the past. The heroes of these novels hold a vision of a future utopia; that utopia will evolve from the past struggles described in the novels. This is perhaps an imaginative evasion; our literature skirts present anguish by appealing to a past fraught with greater problems that were nonetheless surmounted. To gaze upon a troubling past offers an implicit recognition of the progress made since then. Many of these works contain a moment of prophetic vision of a greater future. Often the vision is one of an unspecified Canadian reality; sometimes the vision is more universal.

The best-known historical novelist of this period is Thomas B. Costain (1885–1965). Like Gilbert Parker's, Costain's literary career gained him a solid position in New York, the literary centre. In one of his best-sellers, *High Towers* (1949), a saga of the Le Moyne family, Costain described the history of Canada; his hero glimpsed a heavenly city in a transformed continent. The novel offers a reassuring vision of English-speaking hegemony as the fulfillment of what the French explorers had sought:

> You know what the old maps were like — all around the lands of the earth the waters of four oceans, and above the oceans a thick mist. The mist has been pierced in the West! . . . I . . . see this land teeming with cities . . . with towers rising higher than the Rock of Quebec. I've never been able to see what flag flies over these great high cities. It may not be the flag of France any more than that of England or Spain. Perhaps it will be the colors of a new race. But that won't mean defeat for us who dream now of keeping the fleur-de-lis over all the new continent. What we are doing may be a part of something much greater, the nature of which we can't yet forsee.

The imagery of the darkness over the waters pierced by the light of knowledge comes from Genesis and places this prophecy in very exacting company. The imagery also distances the book from any troublesome thoughts about what might be happening in the streets at the bottom of those skyscrapers.

Costain carries the affirmation of the new land into the realm of prophecy. Another device used to affirm the new land is the resurrection. This device is used by Thomas Raddall (1903–) in *Hangman's Beach* (1966). Raddall's novels stand out from the rest of the works we are observing in their characterization, plotting and stylistic fluency. They are limited by genre — the adventure story — and by their characters' lack of ethical complexity. They convey the same message as other works described here. For example, *Roger Sudden* (1944) is a swashbuckling story told with considerable economy and verve. But it reminds readers of *The Seats of the Mighty*, where humble participants who refuse to remain pawns can overturn grand schemes. Shift the scene from Quebec to Louisbourg and kill the flawed hero rather than give him his sweetheart; a similar message is contained in both books. Parker thought the fall of New France was a result of moral rot; Raddall attributes it to an obsession with walls, to what we can view metaphorically as a fortress mentality. Raddall's works offer another instance of the moralization of political and military events.

The theme of choice absorbs Raddall. *His Majesty's Yankees* (1942) deals realistically with the business of allegiance to one side or the other. The hero, who is from Nova Scotia, must choose sides during the American Revolution. He notes that while the British authorities in Halifax may be remote, pettifogging and snobbish, the Yankees are aggressive and predatory. He prudently stays with the beeves rather than switching to the stoats. In *Hangman's Beach*, the characters choose to adopt the new land. Slow in its beginnings, the plot deals with the adventures of Michel Cascamond, French prisoner-of-war confined in Halifax from 1807 to 1812. Cascamond seeks liberty. He also wants to marry Ellen Dewar. Her protector is entrepreneur Peter McNab, who lives on an island in the harbour. He attempts to set himself in former times and to divorce his domestic life from the reality of his business concerns, a step the author accepts uncritically, although McNab's pretensions grow incompatible with the demands of the commercial practices supporting them. The novel describes Halifax in a peak of wartime prosperity, and McNab reigns as a sort of wise old godfather who evades the various embargoes that threaten his business with no loss of money or moral standing.

The novel describes Cascamond the prisoner; his love, with her ambiguous social status; and Cascamond's rival, who governs the prison system in which Cascamond languishes. The novel concludes with McNab helping Cascamond and Ellen escape to Acadia, where they can dwell peacefully among the French Canadians. In the novel, Cascamond tries to escape by posing as a corpse that will be taken outside the prison and buried. Buried he is. He must be buried in a manner that convinces the guards accompanying the burial detail, and it is with difficulty that he extracts himself from the damp earth of the grave. His resurrection appears to him "as if he had indeed risen from the dead, with a completely new life before him." This life, after further vicissitudes, he will live in the new land.

McNab's island, in Halifax harbour, has been blighted from the novel's beginning. A British admiral had erected a gibbet, from which those executed for naval offenses dangle as a warning to others. At the novel's end, McNab's henchmen tear down the horrid thing. "Hangman's Beach" becomes an item in a tourist brochure. The life-affirming, commercial society McNab exemplifies has purged itself of its gloomy associations, and Cascamond and Ellen are saved. In a prefatory note, the author calls the book a romance, and so it is. Prisons, gibbets and revenge yield to the triumph of life. The evocation of the new land poses itself against starkly opposing forces.

Another familiar theme is the threat posed to the good society by enemy forces, outer and inner. Thus we have invasion novels. In English Canada, they are often about the war of 1812. They can be very bad indeed, as "Ralph Connor" (Charles William Gordon) demonstrates in *The Runner* (1929). Connor combines a superman hero, René La Flamme, and a faithful Indian companion, Black Hawk, in a series of incidents that includes every Family Compact myth about the war in Upper Canada. Threat novels in general allow writers to discuss their every bias and to create enemies of unadulterated malevolence. The novels face in two directions. First, they imply that because threats have been overcome before, new threats will also be overcome. Yet at the same time, the threat is never fully scotched; evil forces seem ever willing to renew the struggle. For the most part, the novels in this category defy analysis. Look, for example, at *The Mac's of '37* (1910), by "Price–Brown" (Eric Bohn). What is to be done with a set of secret caves along the St. Lawrence where a would-be Jacobite laird attempts to reconstruct a bygone way of life? At least John Richardson, who used a similar refuge device in a novel nearly eighty years earlier, had the good sense of plunk his hideout in the middle of the Scottish Highlands rather than along an important trade route. Or look at Robert Sellar's *Morven* (1911) and *Hemlock* (1918). The author's anti-Catholic, anti-French-Canadian prejudices show when he causes the habitant militia at Chateauguay to flee the scene of battle.[4] Or, finally, ponder A. L. Davis's *The Old Loyalist* (1908), which is a call to arms against all sorts of enemies. The book is set during the Fenian Raids in 1865. Yet it refers to "Dagoes."

Readers are told of the need to keep the Anglo-Saxon race in good shape. And the book's hero has an old black servant, whom he teases with tales of Fenian atrocities. In the novel, every alternative to "white Canada" is to be resisted. Threat novels also have their mainstream echoes. Sara Jeanette Duncan's *The Imperialist* (1904) may be one of the finest novels in Canada written before 1920. Yet its hero excoriates the United States as "the light woman among nations, welcoming all comers, mingling her pure blood." A cultural threat induces a racist response in many of these novels. Thus the novel of assimilation is often set in the past, when the make-up of the immigrant was beyond reproach. The threat novel is with us still, in the fiction of Margaret Atwood (*The Edible Woman, Surfacing*) and Richard Rohmer (*Ultimatum*). Joseph Choquet's *Under Canadian Skies* (1922) presents a final solution to a threat: its two lovers flee the events of 1837 to seek refuge under American skies.[5] Acadia offers another version of the threat, and English– and French-Canadian novelists wage a distanced debate. Albert Laurent's *L'épopée tragique* (1956) rehearses the material of Napoléon Bourassa ninety years after the fact. Again, sexually aggressive British officers harass pure *Acadien* heroines; epic and Scriptural imagery enhance the stature of a suffering people; and villainy speaks but one language. Laurent adds a new twist when he discards the image of the Acadians as passive endurers. He creates Paul Brault, who transforms himself into a guerrilla leader, "Le Tuer." Laurent's Acadians may resemble Bourassa's in that they undergo a "chemin de croix," but they also "n'etaient pas aussi moutons que l'histoire les dépeint généralement." The English-Canadian version of this threat views it the other way. Sir Charles G. D. Roberts' *The Raid from Beauséjour* (1894) and *A Sister to Evangeline* (1898), Raddall's *Roger Sudden* and Evelyn Eaton's *The Sea Is So Wide* (1943) depict English settlements beleaguered by a potential fifth column. Eaton's novel contains a series of mediators, good English people who resist the aims of their leaders but are powerless to halt them.

These novels demonstrate that the fiction of threat can exist alongside the fiction of reassurance: what one side sees as malevolence is, to the other side, bad planning. Generally, the mood in the books is one of national reconciliation and the optimism that accompanies it. An example is an English-Canadian novel of the period, *Leopard and Lily* (1935) by John Hodgson (1892– ?). The hero, Dieudon, is French-born, yet loyal to the English. He wins the French-Canadian Marguerite Valois after a number of incredible escapades. After the conquest, the hero is rewarded with a colonelcy in the Royal Canadian Militia; he also receives a share of the fabled "Treasure of Montcalm," which he has helped locate, and is given a seignory as well. The book might appear to be an especially tawdry English-Canadian fantasy of reconciliation and profit. Yet it differs from other potboilers because it tries to be more than a good yarn.[6]

A French-Canadian novel of this period touches upon the same theme. Robert Laroque de Roquebrune (1889–1978) won the French Prix David in 1923 for his *Les habits rouges*, a novel set in 1837. The subject could have called forth the strongest of exclusionist messages. Instead, it is shaped into a instance of pain and loss that serves no one's benefit. The novel is formally innovative. Events are presented in a realistic manner. In the book, a familiar subject is handled in a new way and with new techniques.

Les habits rouges is not concerned with choice. Choice implies the repudiation of one national alternative in favour of another. In this novel, the characters have taken positions before the action begins; they do not budge from their roles. They lack the luxury of choice. They are not free to agonize during decisive moments; instead, as in real life, they are swept along. The decisiveness of a moment becomes apparent after it has passed. Yet the author walks a thin line: he refuses his characters that degree of self-knowledge and determination that marks heroically conceived characters. But he does not present a group of puppets who lack free will.

Before the novel opens, Jérôme de Thavenet and Lieutenant Armontgorry have made some choices. *Canadien* they may be, but both wear the Queen's uniform. They have both fallen in love with Lilian Colborne, the daughter of a man who figured prominently in the suppression of the 1837 Rebellion. One character in the book condemns such unions because they produce "une race illégitime, race intermédiare qui venait s'interposer entre les deux peuples ennemies." This "middle ground," viewed with hostility by both sides, is crushed, although the book is filled with ambiguities and complex alliances. Jérôme's sister Henriette falls in love with a redcoat, Lieutenant Fenwick; English officers differ among themselves over the degree of severity with which the social unrest should be handled. Henriette is caught between an admiration for the cause of Papineau and his associates and a distaste for their personalities. One of them, an English-speaking *patriote*, falls for her.

The process of political violence defines and polarizes this welter of ambiguities. The redcoated *Canadiens* are trapped between the two sides. When they attempt to join the *patriote* cause, one is shot, the other exiled. Lieutenant Fenwick and another character are killed in battle. Henriette sides with the *patriotes* and escapes. At the end of the novel, she stands alone and without choice because of the choices others have made.

Roquebrune was uneasy with the situation he created, as one incident indicates. During the fight at St.-Charles, Henriette takes up a gun and helps defend the rebel position. She experiences "une volupté étrange," which "lui faisait battre" her heart. When the Anglophone *patriote* Brown, who has sought her love, attempts to flee, she shoots and kills him. What are readers to make of this? Henriette has not been presented as an Amazon.

Is her act an aberration or a coming–of–age? We do not know. Present-day feminists might think she is just another soldier doing her job, though surely that impresses our own notions upon a novel written in the twenties. The unexplained nature of the event leaves us puzzled. The author has given Henriette a choice in her allegiance to the rebels. He takes that choice to a logical conclusion. Then he pauses. He fails to integrate that act with the rest of the novel. The ethical dilemmas prove too difficult to sort out.

Another incident also shows his unease. Armontgorry realizes that events are forcing him to make choices he would rather avoid. He rides away in his red coat from a riot between two increasingly pugnacious sides. As he rides, the falling snow covers him and he fades into the atmosphere. The specific identity of one character disappears in the face of a historical process that reduces individuals to anonymity. Loyalties fade or are compromised. Henriette smuggles a *patriote* through the English lines; she becomes a warrior, then a loner, despite conventional expectations about the heroine's role in a historical novel.

Distinctions between the characters grow blurred as expected roles and allegiances fade into the death, imprisonment or solitude that overtakes them all. The Englishman is unable to gain the hand of the *canadienne*; death causes his spurning. Tribal distinctions have been maintained but at the cost of useless suffering. The historical process turns individuals into tragic shapes. True, no one escapes the consequences of wearing a red coat, yet common humanity has directed all the characters, whatever their colours, to a similar destination. This is a very new spirit in the historical novel in Canada.

Roquebrune was not to maintain this novel thrust. A later novel, *D'un océan à l'autre* (1924), presents the building of the CPR in episodic fashion that recalls a Cinerama spectacle of the 1950s. The history of the CPR develops a sense of the split between the two founding peoples, and of Riel, his execution and all that entailed. Riel, Big Bear and the rebellions appear in Roquebrune's book, but he brushes away these divisive elements. Père Lacombe, a missionary who played an equivocal role in the events, reflects as he rides the newly completed road:

> Le rail collait bien à cette terre de l'Ouest et nul ne pourrait l'en arracher. Le vent des prairies serait désormais déchiré par le sifflet strident des locomotives. Le Canada faisait un bond gigantesque et allait prendre possession de son domaine merveilleux de l'Atlantique au Pacifique.

The missionary's vision of reconciliation ignores the brutality that went into the road's creation. *D'un océan à l'autre* ignores human conflict; the mountains and hills are made low, but at the expense of a compelling perspective.

Les habits rouges showed that the fossilization of the historical novel could not continue indefinitely; other novels began to show that the traditionally optimistic messages were darkening. A new spirit began to be expressed in the themes — though not always in the formal structures — of these novels.

III

Hindsight asserts the beginnings of a new spirit, but some caution is required: Canadian historical novels did not suddenly burst forth from their fossilization after 1923. Occasionally, though, a historical novel would be so well-written that it could be assessed as a fiction. Two such books were written by Grace Campbell (1895–1963). Campbell's *Thorn-Apple Tree* (1942) and *The Higher Hill* (1944) are set in a distant pioneer past; they describe rural idylls. Beautifully illustrated by Franklin Carmichael, they relate domestic events in which a couple's courage and trust in each other enable them to surmount life's obstacles. The husband marches off to fight at Lundy's Lane; he returns a few pages later to recount his adventures. History is used as a distraction from the domestic struggles shaping the novels. Another idyll with a historical setting, a domestic drama set in the past, is Robert J. C. Stead's *The Homesteaders* (1916). Stead (1880–1959) allows elements of the historical novel and the dark rural idyll to collide with the conventions of melodrama and adventure fiction. The book begins as a historical novel, its theme the threat material prosperity poses to pioneering idealism; it concludes with a set of pulp-fiction formulas and includes the obligatory Mountie. Some books in the *Jalna* series also are set in the past; they are another example of the blending of the historical with the idyllic.

While these works were being written, another process was occurring. It is exemplified in two novels by Maida Parlow French, *Boughs Bend Over* (1943) and *All This To Keep* (1947). The books describe, with many homely details, a pioneer family's struggles in Upper Canada in the years before 1812. The family's fight against poverty, exile and price-gouging, land-stealing speculators springs from its historical situation. The family confronts a dishonest half-pay officer whom the imperial system has placed over them. The books offer a glimpse of a pioneering reality that does not stress a common unity and purpose threatened only by outside enemies and traitorous insiders. Instead, French shows how lives are shaped by the systems created to deal with historical catastrophes, such as the exile of those who were loyal to the King during the Revolution. Out of that conflict emerges a new entity, which is both imperfect and committed to its new territory. Yet the attentive reader derives no easy reassurance from these novels. The battle is neither entirely won nor really over.

These two books contain no prophetic vision, once obligatory in the historical novel. Many other novels also omit assurance or prophetic vision. Three of them, written by Mabel Dunham (1881–1957), withold the comforts of future reassurance set in the past. *The Trail of the Conestoga* (1924), *Toward Sodom* (1927) and *The Trail of the King's Men* (1931) describe events in Upper Canada and the thirteen colonies from 1776 to after 1867, although they are not set in chronological order. The first novel presents an idyll set in the past; the Niagara River is the new Jordan for Loyalist seekers of the promised land. The third novel describes the family's flight to Upper Canada and the political upheavals that their emigration caused. Its message is familiar: the Loyalists performed what they "knew was right . . . and that is all that really matters."

The middle novel is the disturbing one. It could pass for an English-Canadian version of a French-Canadian *roman de la terre*. Once settled, the promised land develops the structures of modernity, in which the family unit can no longer maintain a satisfactory existence. A son concludes a misspent youth by fleeing to New York and dying in a train wreck. Another character flourishes in politics and insurance and is lost to the farm. A third heads west to prepare the way for Russian Mennonites (the family's origins are Pennsylvania Dutch). Despite the novel's idyllic opening, the intrusion of the modern world wrecks the tightly knit family.

Another writer whose vision was bleak was West Coast novelist Frederick Niven (1878–1944), who set three novels in British Columbia:[7] *The Flying Years* (1935), *Mine Inheritance* (1940) and *The Transplanted* (1944). Again, the novels are not chronological. The first, which begins before the Riel Rebellion and ends after the Great War, presents an ambivalent view about the onset of white civilization in the British Columbia interior. Repeatedly, the novel calls attention to the callousness and greed with which Indian claims were brushed aside. Niven describes the rapidity with which change, in the form of white culture and technology, moved in the West. He is made uneasy by that rapidity. The title indicates this, as does his description of a bustling white economic system that carries all before it:

> The miserable business was over, Riel hanged, the snow of another winter quaking down over the land, and MacPherson's chief concern in life was whether it should be wheels or runners to carry the wheat of those he called *our progressives* to the grain elevators that had been erected by the side of the railway.

The second novel, *Mine Inheritance*, is more romantic in structure and tone. It slips back in time to Selkirk's colony and repeats a traditional theme: the need to adapt to the new land. It exhibits less imaginative energy than its gloomier predecessor. *The Transplanted*, the third in the series, describes a Scottish immigrant who helped to open the British Columbia interior. He is one of those characters who perform historic acts without ever themselves being aware of it. "It was he who had been responsible for beating back the forests, beating them back." Niven is less hesitant and shows less sense of loss than Dunham, yet both follow equivocation with an over-compensatory affirmation.

Historical fiction began to contain a more complex view of history. Instead of a steady upward climb along the axis of progress, the graph begins to indicate dips and swings. This complexity reaches a significant point in the novels of Léo-Paul Desrosiers (1896–1967). His works signalled an end to the celebratory, romantic tradition of the French-Canadian historical novel. Desrosiers' three finest historical novels — *Nord–sud* (1931), *Les engagés du grand portage* (1938) and *Les opiniâtres* (1941) — display an imagination profoundly *nationaliste* yet unwilling to support a triumphalist interpretation of events.

Les engagés attracted great critical attention and won the Prix David when it appeared. Much of its appeal lies in its shock value. With brutal simplicity, it picks up the myth of the heroism and high adventure of the fur trade and shakes it as a burglar would a noisy dog. The book describes the rise of Nicolas Montour. He begins as just another hand in a canoe, then becomes a partner in the company. He builds his success upon lies, bluff and brutality. Montour retains the skills of the clever but unprepossessing schemer who knows how to play the system.

Desrosiers broke new ground in his portrayal of the system. He acknowledges that men worked in the fur trade to make money—not to plant Bibles. In Desrosiers' novel, the system is bureaucratically organized. Its factors are sent, like tax farmers, to remote locations to obtain enough profit to satisfy the expectations of the central managers. The system has no conscience. It is competitive; it demoralizes its Indian suppliers and consumers and it brutalizes its hired help. Desrosiers presents in detail the hardships of the post-Conquest voyageurs: the unremitting labour, the wretched working conditions caused by climate and terrain, the bad food, the isolation, the loneliness and the pace at which labour must be carried out if the competitive edge is to be maintained. The senior partner, Tom MacDonald (called "Bandylegs" behind his back), knows Montour's nature, yet continues to promote him. The system judges by results rather than character.

The book seems in some respects a thirties, anti-business novel set in the past. The bosses are *anglais* and the workers *canadien*. This single-mindedness proves the novel's weak point. The partners are so greedy, the workmen so brutalized and stupid, the competition so ruthless that Montour's rise is foreseeable. The novel contains convincing detail about work conditions, portaging and the ins and outs of negotiating with the Indians. Its weakness is its primitive psychology, by which Montour appears forever able to fool everyone. All men are either dupes, or honest but powerless to halt the resolute schemer. Louison Turenne is one good man who resists Montour's wiles, only to find himself increasingly isolated. One incident between the two men reveals the weaknesses I have mentioned.

Necessity has made Turenne wary of Montour. We are told that Turenne lacks Montour's "psychologie pratique," an ability to "[p]arler à chacun son langage, connaître la façon de lui plaire, de l'irriter, de le rallier à ses projets." Such talents enable Montour to seduce others in his schemes to overthrow a competitor: "connaissant de manière réaliste le caractère de trois ou quatre personnes, il lancera d'un oreille de la premiere une parole qui rebiondira de l'une à l'autre et ira accomplir au loin l'effet prévu." Yet we recall a moment from a few pages earlier, when Montour sought to catch Turenne in his toils. The moment is a rather unsubtle discourse on the money that can be made by a man tough-minded enough to do what is necessary. The author is unable to dramatize convincingly the skills of his anti-hero. We are not shown Montour's prowess as a schemer, we are told of it. Thus his rise seems foreordained.

The novel has some strengths. The English-run system is corrupt, yet we are given no inkling that things were any different under French control. The tribe is not excused by the introduction of wicked outsiders. The novel subjects romance to naturalistic treatment; the historical novelist's imagination need no longer be limited by the upbeat themes that had sustained it. (Unremitting pessimism might create its own orthodoxy.)

A critic noted that *Les engagés* offers "probably the best introduction to the whole northern myth."[8] For "introduction" I would substitute "demolition." *Nord–sud*, on the other hand, introduces and modifies another set of nationalist myths. At first glance *Nord–sud* seems to be another *roman de la terre*, the back-to-the-land fiction so important in the French-Canadian literary enterprise.[9] Set in 1848, the novel is about a dilemma: how to find space sufficient to accommodate the needs of a burgeoning agricultural population? In *Jean Rivard, le défricheur* (1874), Gérin-Lajoie's solution, supported by Church and State alike, had been colonization. Open up new areas of Quebec to cultivation and the rural population would stop moving to Montreal and the mill towns of New England. In *Nord–sud*, Vincent Douaire is tempted by California, where the gold rush is underway. He shuns the promises of colonization and goes to

California. The warning to him and others that "vous deviendrez anglais et protestants" fails to stop Vincent; he follows the call of the *pays d'en haut* that marked New France from its beginnings: "Il écoutait l'appel des hommes qui vivent sous le ciel, errent en liberté, nomades comme des Indiens." The French authorities sought to restrain the force they saw as a threat to the colony's strength; the new dispensation also condemned it. The break-up of the rural society and the end of an agrarian Quebec seems to bother Desrosiers less than it did the clerisy trying to maintain an agrarian way of life.

The novel is about the onset of modernity, the drive toward individual fulfillment, which disregards the weakening effect it has on the collectivity. Still, the book bears a deceptive resemblance to *Les anciens Canadiens*, in its evocation of a host of rural customs and traditions. Nostalgia pervades *Les anciens Canadiens*. *Nord–sud* resembles a museum rather than a lost treasure-chest. It does not inspire or lament: it illustrates and classifies. The novel shows the texture of a culture that will be swept away under the pressures of modernization. Young peoples' courting clubs and games, a story-teller who relates the plot of a blood–and–thunder thriller, *Ner Bourdeau*, a militia drill, the seasonal cycles of work, lengthy accounts of scenery: Desrosiers captures these in his portrait of a past world. But he did not write a thriller; romantic nostalgia is not his purpose. Vincent is neither condemned nor praised for his departure. He tries to stay in Quebec, attempting to join a colonization group. His spirit keeps pushing him on, even at the expense of abandoning the woman he loves. Throughout, Desrosiers remains objective.

One critic noted that "Desrosiers a toujours été plus heureux dans l'invention que dans l'exécution."[10] In *Nord–sud*, no subtle psychology is imprinted upon Vincent: he is the restless young man of story, legend and fact. In this novel, important things take place around Vincent. His society, which faces a mortal threat, is going about its business, as people do in the face of lingering catastrophe. The community continues its traditional pursuits.

The book is an account of communal disruption within a thoroughly realized historical setting, and its author reverses the traditional strategies of historical fiction writers, especially French-Canadian writers. Nostalgia has yielded to detailed description; objective accounts of actions replace ideological presentations of character; complex and ambiguous conclusions replace univocal conclusions. *Nord–sud* displays a fine imagination at work; Desrosiers was content to leave to the reader the task of figuring out the meaning of the story.

Desrosiers was a figurehead for the imaginative forces that were changing the shape of historical fiction. *Les engagés* took the stuff of romance and turned it into naturalism; the story insisted upon a material rather than an ideal basis for the historical process. *Nord–sud* removed the pretty frame from the rural idyll; readers placed the experience in whatever context they chose. Desrosiers' third book, *Les opinâtres*, contains the central motif of French-Canadian nationalism, *la survivance*, and finds there a mixture of values rather than unalloyed good. Set during the period when New France lay exposed to the Iroquois threat, the novel tells the story of one couple. Desrosiers restates frequently the theme of an indifferent mother country, yet he also strips away the glamour from the struggle to survive. Pierre de Rencontre and his wife, Ysabau, want to be settlers. In other novels, such a desire would constitute their attachment to the new land. They attempt to settle on a farm, yet they shrink at the perpetual Iroquois threat. Pierre spends more time fighting Indians than farming. Their sons grow up and the fight continues. Finally a fleet of troops arrives in Quebec, signalling an end to France's inaction. The response: "Mais tous ceux qui, comme Pierre, avaient longtemps récu dans l'enfer de cette angoisse ne pouvaient ni regarder, ni crier, ils pleuraient."

Though this novel lacks the power of the other two, it points out Desrosiers' willingness to play with convention. The convention is the family's struggles. In other historical fiction, the historical process is something far away, a distraction from the main event. In Desrosiers' book, the family's battle symbolizes the colony's battle. Pierre and Ysabau venture to the land they seek to cultivate, yet they fail to find peace. When she arrives at her new home on the frontier, Ysabau is frightened at the closeness of man to nature — a rational response. The Iroquois are an animated part of that wilderness and its pervasive hostility. In this typical North American primal encounter, nature must be tamed rather than freed.

The family's experience is also mixed. One son joins a fur brigade. He does not lead the conventional life of glorious adventure; instead, he is exposed to corruption. Desrosiers emphasizes the grim side of the struggle to survive. His changing of the thematic conventions is often accompanied by a sharp sense of the complexity of experience. *Nord–sud* refuses to weep for the lost culture and to cheer for the new culture; it demands a more complex response from the reader than does either the rural idyll or the rural lament. Similarly, when Desrosiers describes the pain and loss of *la survivance*, our response is shaded.

A sense of Desrosiers' uniqueness comes from examining two other novels. Pierre Benoit (1906–) wrote two books, *Martine Juillete, fille du roi* (1945) and *Le Marchand de la place royale* (1960). The novels tell of the generations of the Guillaumin family from New France's beginnings to the conquest. A bald recital of events in the family would sound like a catalogue of disasters. The perils of pioneer life take their toll. In the first novel, the unfriendly forces are the Iroquois and the indifference of the French authorities. A legendary Frontenac (found in many historical novels) removes the Indian threat. [11] Toward the end of the book, the heroine has a vision of the endurance of France in North America. By her motherhood, she has helped to bring this future: "c'était les fruits de la vie, ces enfants qui assureraient la survivance du patrimonie séculaire sur la sol adoptif." Martine's motherhood is paralleled by the spiritual motherhood of Marguerite Bourgeoys, who acts as a saving force throughout the novel. Through her compassion, Marguerite makes possible the union of a *canadien* with an Indian woman.

The second novel contains a different set of enemies. The English remain firmly in the background, but at the end of the book they triumph. François-Xavier, a descendant of the Guillaumin family, is the title character. Before he dies he delivers a prophecy, composed of melancholy reflections on the fate of New France. François-Xavier and French Montreal expire together. Yet the two novels depict many examples of grit and endurance. These positive forces cannot be separated from the forces that cause the colony's downfall. Bigot appears as the alien, metropolitan force that stunts New France. One of François-Xavier's sons becomes disgraced through his involvement with La Friponne and the Bigot circle. Bigot stands for the forces leading to the colony's fall. Though he may trap some of the weaker colonists, the insiders endure. Other traditional motifs appear as well: for example, the hero resists the seductions of a woman from France and weds first an Indian woman and then a *canadienne* widow.

Benoit's world is not as sharply binary as the world created by a novelist-pamphleteer like Marmette, but it lacks the complexity of Desrosiers'. Frustration and exhaustion in one writer's works become heroic endurance in another's. The tortured weeping of Pierre at the end of *Les opiniâtres* is an emblem of the costs of the struggle. This bite is missing from the pathetic deathbed of François Xavier.

The novels discussed in this section introduce a sense of pain into the novelization of the historical process. The books do not leave their readers with a sense of crises surmounted; they deal instead with a set of problems coped with in a more or less successful fashion. The novels do not provide limitless futures; instead, they offer a limited past whose hopes and dreams are not necessarily secured forever by the novels' events. These books add a new dimension to the depiction of history. I use the term "realism" to denote a kind of moral complexity, an attitude that shuns ideal creations in which good and evil are quite separate and discernible. In this sense, the novels of Desrosiers are realistic in tone and narrative convention.

IV

Two novels sum up the complexities of the period. They treat similar experiences, deliver similar messages and present a mixture of the innovative and the traditional. Philip Child (1898–1978) wrote what could be seen as the historical romance to end all historical romances. His novel, *The Village of Souls*, is romantic because it follows the logic of dream rather than of reason, and is thus close to the essence of romance. Because sadness and suffering mark the book, its emotional tone is "realistic." Traditional in its theme, it remains innovative in the extremity of its romantic form, a new method for dealing with history.

The book is about a voyageur whose adventures circle around the most enduring theme: choice. The spiritual struggle takes pride of place here. The village of the title is the ghostly village the forest Indians saw as the afterlife, the place to which death brings us all.

The location seems better suited to a psychological novel than to a historical novel, and the book does not describe history as we usually think of it. The book is dotted with real names: Marguerite de Bourgeoys, Marie de l'Incarnation, Father Bernard and Mme de la Peltrie. Things happen here that the histories confirm: young men in New France desert the farms and villages for the *pays d'en haut*; Indians terrorize whites in an attempt to preserve their territory; white diseases decimate Indian tribes; young women without dowries are sent out as *filles du roi* to help populate a colony. Quebec, Montreal, Lake Superior, the Mississippi: these are real places that still exist. Yet all these events and places appear as real items in a dream. How can that dream be history?

Consider the novel's handling of space and time. The second edition begins with a vague definition of location: "*pays d'en haut, 1665.*"[12] By the second chapter, we know the characters are canoeing through the Thousand Islands, but the author intends (since the first edition had no heading) to leave the reader puzzled at the novel's opening. Once we pass beyond Quebec and Montreal, we are in relatively undifferentiated space. Perhaps the novelist was careless about the sort of detail necessary to historical fiction. But I think the author's vagueness is consonant with the spatial experience the novel seeks to relate.

Time also suffers its dislocations, at least time as the characters experience it. It is difficult to construct a chronology of the book's events. There are a few statements about the heroine's age when a catastrophe changed her life, and we are told that she and the hero, Bertrand Jornay, met a month before the novel opens. Calendrical measurements are sparse; the characters tell time by the seasons. Someone notes a seasonal alteration in the landscape; a character huddles in winter captivity; as the novel concludes, rain is changing into snow. The journey (the novel is composed of journeys; the pun hidden in the hero's name is obvious) that ends the book comes immediately upon this time of snow and rain, scarcely a prudent period for a long canoe trip. Seasonal change is harnessed to the characters' emotional states.

This play with space and time exists within a melodramatic narrative context. Jornay, a voyageur raised in the slums of Paris, contracts a marriage with Lys de Faverolles, one of the *filles du roi* brought to new France. She was brought up by her gentleman–adventurer father, and is imprisoned and branded as a prostitute. She did not choose New France, but rather ended up there. Jornay wants to help his new wife escape the colony she loathes. By chance, he rescues the Indian Anne from captivity. She is later schooled briefly by the Ursuline sisters. Jornay's mixed-blood partner, Titange, schemes to possess Lys. He bribes some hostile Indians, who abduct her. Anne loves Jornay, and accompanies him on an expedition to locate Lys. On the expedition, he contracts a bigamous marriage with Anne.

Lys passes her time in captivity by nursing plague-stricken Indians. Jornay and Anne find her in a dying village near Lake Superior; Lys is also dying. She secretly poisons herself so that Jornay may marry Anne, who has disappeared. After a close brush with death, Jornay locates Anne. They resolve to journey to the heart of the continent.

The Village of Souls is a novel about choice. In the novel, Jornay's decision to choose a Canadian reality is purchased at the price of Lys's life. The novel is not realistic in tone: arrivals and departures follow narrative necessity rather than plausibility.

Child's novel is modernist in its presentation of inward dramas through outward couplings and exchanges, in its use of two wastelands (the dying village and the empty swamp where Jornay almost perishes) and in its emotional bleakness. Yet it still manages to take the Canadian historical novel back to its Gothic beginnings. As the writers of the American South demonstrate in this century, Gothicism and modernism are quite compatible. Child wrote a fiction of ambivalence, of splits, guilt and hauntings.[13] In its handling of the theme of choice and its reliance upon dream and vision, the novel presents a kind of psycho-history. It can be seen as a meditation on the costs of Canadian citizenship. From the beginning, Lys is the victim. Jornay first sees her in Montreal, where a Mohawk captive is being tortured. It is the death-and-the-maiden motif of Romantic archetype; Lys is the etherealized, passive female who cannot survive the grim environment into which she falls.

Anne is another stereotype: the tomboy, the woman whose sexuality is never in question but whose vigour and rage are seen as "masculine" qualities. She is savage (she castrates a captive), active (she fights for

Jornay when Lys is too terrified to move) and fleshly (Jornay first takes her in a loveless assault, then comes to maturity in the sexuality she offers him). The two women live in a world of violence and death; they are like active and passive versions of a woman who lives in a terrorized world.

Infernal imagery underlines the mood of terror in the novel. Birds shriek "demoniacally" and fires shade characters' faces in hellish hues. Hell is everywhere: in the stricken Indian villages, in fiery torture scenes, in the wastelands that nearly absorb Jornay. The wilderness may at first seem to be a sub-world but it flourishes as a genuine world. The terror it contains dwells in the town as well. Neither offers a refuge from what haunts the characters and from the dilemmas they must resolve.

Jornay is a strange hero, at once passive and spasmodically active. He is brutal in his assault upon Anne; then he withdraws into his cabin as guilt catches up with him. His near-death in the swamp is both a rite of purgation, the sort of ordeal a romantic hero must undergo, and also a device for the author to give Jornay something decisive to do. One woman has killed for him, another has killed herself for him. He must perform some action that redeems him. In the last scene in the novel, Mornay is paddling his canoe as Anne rests in it.

The characters are at times stereotypical in their behaviour; they remain bearable because of the novel's dream-like consistency. The final river journey seems to indicate faith in the power of romantic love, but that faith is not supported by the ambivalences of the text. The novel is filled with overt dreaming; the final implicit wish-fulfillment fantasy passes almost unnoticed. Lys's ethereality links her to the night-world. Her final appearance is in a vision. Anne has a dream in which she recalls the moment of the white man's arrival in the big ships. Jornay knows she could not have witnessed the event, and attributes the dream to the confused recollections of Anne's mother, a Spanish captive. (The vision makes sense as an example of the collective recovery of the past.) On two occasions, the missionary Father Bernard theorizes about dreaming. To him, dreams do not oppose waking life, but assist us in integrating a hidden self with our public self. Child's novel conveys a united world by stressing the things common to both heroines, despite their many differences.

Jornay first sees Lys against a background of torture and death, the world Anne springs from. Anne had some education at the hands of the Ursulines, and thus is not as remote from Lys's world as first appears. Early in the novel, Anne's wrists are scarred from rawhide burnings; Lys had been handcuffed when she first boarded ship for New France and she bears the scars of her branding. One scene in the novel places the two women in an emblem of unity amid superficial diversity.

Inside the hut at Teiomhouskwaronte wood smoke as sweet and pungent as incense, warmth, the illusion of security; outside a gale out of a mackerel sky, tossing an aspen bough against the single window, sending shoals of sere leaves furiously rattling against the walls and along the roof in their descent to mould. An arrow of light from the west entered the window and cut the interior into two limbos of murk in one of which Lys sat with a blanket about her shoulders squaw-fashion, not distinguishable in the poor light from the figure of Anne crouching in Indian isolation in the opposite gloom.

"Incense," "illusion," "poor light," "gloom," "limbo of murk": these form a hallucinatory atmosphere. Inside and outside are sharply demarcated. The "arrow of light" seems to divide the room, but instead it creates identical portions. Within each of these crouches a version of Woman, yet their postures and the atmosphere itself join them together in mutual solitude.

What is Jornay's choice? He chooses a wild environment, yet Lys's forgiveness and self-sacrifice form the softest break with the mother country imaginable. It is an exhilarating and incredible picture of post-Colonial reconciliation, a thoroughly Canadian fantasy in which the garden is reconciled with the wilderness. *The Village of Souls* attempts to reconcile the self with the burdens of love and the burdens of the wilderness.

The novel is both modernist and traditional. It is modernist in its preoccupation with a world of terror and dreaming, the darkening trend this chapter has been at pains to locate. It is traditional in its faith in the power of romantic love. The novel is filled with modernist devices: waste lands, split heroes, violence, ambiguity. It is also replete with relics of Romantic art: Jornay's upbringing in underworld Paris, Lys's branded shoulder and so on. The novel places its hero in a middle state; his struggles and final night journey end when all his warring impulses are reconciled. In this novel, the ideal is a person who can strengthen personal resolve in the face of infinite horizons. That Romantic quest still defines much of our national culture.

The Village of Souls sums up many of the conflicting currents this chapter has been examining. Louis Vaczek's *River and Empty Sea* does this as well, but in a very different fashion. The novel seems in many ways a waking version of Child's dream.[14] Its hero, Paul Denys, Sieur de St. Simon, is based on a historical figure. He leaves his comfortable life as secretary to Jean Talon to accompany an expedition to Hudson's Bay. The rigours of the journey weld him to the wilderness. He has a son by an Indian woman who later dies. He marries a *canadienne* and assumes proprietorship of his seignory, yet he continues to relish his time in the harsher world of the forest. *River and Empty Sea* deals with the choices posed by the Canadian environment and exemplifies them through sexual selection. The novel contains few stirring events; changes in the hero are conveyed through processes, rather than through dramatic reverses. The novel contains a welter of convincing detail—about the fur trade, wilderness dining, climate, terrain, Indian customs and missionary enterprises. The detail indicates how realistic in technique the book is.

The two novels occupy different points on a continuum; they offer realistic or romantic treatments of similar themes. Child's Jornay can be fitted easily into the model of a modernist hero in his restlessness, his ambivalence, his capacity for cruelty and his eagerness to pass through stark landscapes on his continual quest. Vaczek's Denys bears the same profile, though his quest begins as a romantic one and concludes with an existentialist note. A young man in search of adventure, he also seeks to elicit a set of values from the landscape. He is initially disgusted by the discomforts of the expedition; its bad food and smells, its fatigue and discomfort are presented in a lively fashion. His self-respect and his search for some moment of significance in the wilderness push him to continue. As he gazes from a lookout point over the Saguenay, he beholds a vision of the forces of nature. He sees both their duality and the stronger force that reconciles them. The prospect he beholds consists of sky blended with water: the two appear to him as a unified vastness. Its boundaries are the woods in the foreground and a beach in the middle distance. Two cloud formations, an expression of duality, drift across the sky, but unity proves the more lasting impression. This strongly moralized landscape parallels the development of the hero: he begins to grow less intent on his own comfort and less scornful of his companions. Yet the duality of experience impresses him, so that what he sees from the lookout is not necessarily what we see. He is still aware of his role as an interloper in the new environment. He still expects to find a message, some sermon in stones, waiting for him. He spends a winter with the expedition and comes to appreciate the simple value of "survival without plan, without laws, without even firm beliefs . . . . " He dreams of a muskrat, then kills one and is given the creature's name, "Acaskwa," by his Indian companions.

In the second part of the novel, Denys reaches the bay and what he trusts will be the mystical revelation he seeks. But the bay does not live up to the promise he imposed upon it; he fails to find what he felt was there. Instead he beholds "an unimaginable wasteland, devoid of all qualities that the human spirit could grasp. It was the reality of eternity before man's mind discovered the Creator." Nature refuses to comfort him, and he is disillusioned.

The end of the novel fails to provide the narrative or psychological

45

interest of the beginning. Denys' search for meaning gave the novel its edge, and thrust it beyond the pat dilemma posed by the choice between the dark heroine and the light one. As the novel progresses, he is increasingly constrained by the colony's rules and flees to the wilderness. He stops running when his mentor, Father Albanel (also based upon a historical figure), convinces Denys that he has not integrated himself into the forest world, that he fled to it out of disgust for the garrison. The novel does not provide a narrative resolution of these metaphysical conflicts.

Before he talks to Father Albanel, Denys returns to the lookout that began his search. The lake is a mirror. "Across its ribbed surface, the wind caught up the snow and flung it about in clouds that spun, racing heedlessly until they vanished." This image of whirling confusion may offer a vision of emptiness: "There was nothing in this dazzling world — no promise, no mystery, not even illusion." Paul refuses to despair. He recognizes the prospect for what it is:

> And yet it was neither empty of spirit nor remote from a man's thoughts. It was simply an immense stretch of snow-covered ice, fringed by dark pines on its near shores, but stretching off in distant snow fogs to the horizon.

Denys' understanding of nature and his response to it ought to settle the novel's philosophical questions: the landscape is what it is, and no attempt to blend with it completely can succeed.

But the novel attempts to satisfy everyone. Denys' Indian wife dies, and he leaves their son to be raised by her tribe. Thus he is free to maintain his wilderness side. He marries his white sweetheart and becomes a prominent colonial official. [15] The need for choice is mitigated by the opportunities for compromise and accommodation that society offers. In the end, Denys is given a month's holiday. His departure provides a final message of integration:

> To Paul the canoe seemed, as much as the sun, an integral part of what was around him. There was no division into separate objects, all were part of an immense and always changing reality: and the sea, far to the north, was a segment of the greater life, its desolation existing in his heart alone.

If the sea's desolation is a value his heart imposes, then how can he and his canoe be as much a part of things as the sun? The author backs away from the drift of his logic and does not provide a statement that would go beyond all those acts of the assertive will by which heroes and heroines bind themselves to a Canadian environment. Instead he seems to say: "The wilderness if necessary, but not necessarily the wilderness."

In his attempt to reconcile the individual to the new environment, Child created a dream-like fable. The conventions of realism seem to work against such a reconciliation. In a realistic novel, the quotidian must always assert itself in the end. Think back to Raddall's *Hangman's Beach*. The adventurous Cascamond takes up a life of domesticity as a schoolmaster. Incredible machinations were needed for his escape from the prison system, yet the refuge he attains seems a commonplace one.

What exactly is the nature of the environment that is being embraced in these novels? The novels return to a landscape that offers sharp dichotomies and imperatives. In the hands of the less talented, the dichotomies are glossed over. In the other novels, history is an arena in which events shake the past even as their results trouble the present.

We can see this clearly in Howard O'Hagan's *Tay John* (1939). Set in historical rather than contemporary time, it is not truly historical fiction because its hero is ultimately mythical. Tay John's acceptance as a white god by the Shuswaps, his slaying of the bear, his self-mutilation, his final apotheosis gained by walking into the earth: all point to a world of myth rather than history. As well, time in the novel is symmetrical. Historically, the landscape is being penetrated by railways; small towns are going up. Amid the modernization, the old, dark hero–gods stalk the earth.

O'Hagan was uneasy about the commitment to a new environment, so Tay John was packed off the stage of history and tucked safely beneath the ground where he could fertilize the growth of legend. In the historical novel, the less mythically conceived figure is bound by time. The time may be prophetic (a character who helped build the great things to come — high towers or national unity), dream-like (Child's Jornay, who sets out on a water journey with a vague goal) or quotidian (a character who picks up life after the struggle and makes daily arrangements). The characters' problems are described in a story that rests upon a sense of a bygone past whose dilemmas may resemble ours but are not the same. The act of artistic creation is mediative. The historical novel's growing gift for locating the point where the myth touches us has become apparent. The next chapter will illustrate how the contemporary historical novel came to share the preoccupations of mainstream fiction.

NOTES

[1] Mary Jean Vipond, *National Consciousness in English-Speaking Canada in the 1920s: Seven Studies* (Diss. Toronto 1974), p. 98.

2 "These pages present a story that took place during the long struggle for Canada that reached its climax in 1759. I might have written a more absorbing volume if I had written about Canada in 2111 A. D. — these dates are equidistant from us. However, our modern astrologers tell us that time–space is curved. I find such a resemblance between 1759 and 1935 that I feel sure the time–sphere has slipped an arc or two." John C. J. Hodgson, Preface, *Lion and Lily, A Story of New France* (Montréal: Renouf, 1935).

3 David M. Hayne, "Angers, Marie-Louise-Félicite'," in William Toye, ed., *Oxford Companion to Canadian Literature* (Toronto: Oxford Univ. Press, 1983), pp. 13–14; Roger Le Moine, "La Sève Immortelle," in Maurice Lemire, ed., II, pp. 1008–13.

4 A catalogue of these prejudices can be found in his *The Tragedy of Quebec. The Expulsion of Its Protestant Farmers*, Intro. by Robert Hill (1907; Toronto: Univ. of Toronto Press, 1974).

5 An interesting aspect of Choquet's novel is its use of a stereotype: the faithful Indian Companion. Choquet's Indian saves the heroine from being raped by a drunken soldier. Three novels assign a major role to Amerinds. In order of worth, they are: Franklin Davey McDowell, *The Champlain Road* (Toronto: Macmillan, 1939); W. D. Lighthall, *The Master of Life* (Toronto: Musson, 1908); and Launcelot Cressy Servos, *Frontenac and the Maid of the Mist* (Toronto: Hal De Gruchy, 1927). The first presents a competent treatment of Huronia and its extinction; though its central characters are a white couple, Huron affairs are integral to the plot. The second connects the destiny of the Five Nations with the help the Indians gave the British in North America. Its chief narrative focus falls on the Indians. To observe that the dialogue of the third is set in doggerel rhyme is to have said it all. These novels indicate that the Tonto stereotype had wearied some writers, though the substitution of Hiawatha for Tonto does not indicate genuine progress.

6 Among the potboilers: Gordon Hill Grahame, *The Bond Triumphant* (Toronto: Hodder & Stoughton, 1923); John M. Elson, *The Scarlet Sash* (Toronto: Dent, 1925); "Johnston Abbot" [Edward Montague Ashworth], *La Roux* (New York: Macmillan, 1924) and *The Seigneurs of La Soulage* (Toronto: Macmillan, 1928); and Louis Arthur Cunningham, *The King's Fool* (Ottawa: Graphic, 1931).

7 Imagine a map of Canada based on historical novels. Some dots would appear around Acadia and Halifax; there would be thick concentrations around central Canada. Rays would reach out from there along the fur-trading routes: south to Louisiana, north to the MacKenzie delta. Another group of dots would mark the prairies and the foothills of the Rockies, concentrating around the regions marked by Selkirk and Riel. The country would stop there, as if Sir John A's railway bribe for leading British Columbia into Confederation had never been consummated. Before the publication of George Bowering's *Burning Water* (1980) and James Houston's *Eagle Song* (1983), Niven's were the only works that would attach British Columbia to the mainland.

48

8 Jack Warwick, "Pays d'en haut," *Culture* (Sept. 1960), pp. 249–502, quoted in "Jugements Critiques," in Léo-Paul Desrosiers, *Les engagés du grand portage*, Presentation et jugements critiques du Maurice Lemire (Montréal: Fides, 1980), p. 229.

9 See M. M. Servais-Maquoi, *Le Roman de la terre au Québec* (Québec: l'Université Laval, 1974); Jeanette Urbas, *From Thirty Acres to Modern Times. The Story of French-Canadian Literature* (Toronto: McGraw-Hill Ryerson, 1976), pp. 9–18; Pierre de Grandpré, *Histoire de la littérature Francaise du Québec*, Tome II, 1900–1945 (Montréal: Librairie Beauchemin, 1968), pp. 115–20.

10 Maurice Lemire, Introduction to Léo-Paul Desrosiers, *Nord–Sud* (Montreal: Fides, 1980), p. 6.

11 For a treatment of the Frontenac of history rather than of legend, see W. J. Eccles, *The Courtier Governor* (Toronto: McClelland and Stewart, [1959]).

12 The second edition of the novel (Toronto: Ryerson, 1948) has the advantage over the first (London: Thornton Butterworth, 1933) not only in terms of availability. It contain's Roloff Beny's evocative black-and-white drawings at the head of each chapter. The texts differ only in slight detail. The final paragraph of the first edition:

He could not know that the phial of mandrake poison which many months ago he had provided for Lys against a different crisis, had served her as a means of death. *Aireskui sutanditenr* [a Huron phrase earlier translated in the novel as "may the unknown God have mercy on us"].

is inserted differently into a paragraph several pages earlier in the 1948 edition:

He did not know that the phial of mandrake poison had served her as a means of death, *Aireskui sutanditenr*.

The second edition divides the final chapter into three rather than two sections; it also includes the information, "Pays d'en Haut, 1665" at the heading of the opening chapter.
   An earlier version of my remarks on *The Village of Souls* appeared in "Fable, Fiction, and Fact: Philip Child's *The Village of Souls*," *Canadian Children's Literature*, No. 23/24 (1981), pp. 59–73.

13 See my "Memory=Pain: The Haunted World of Philip Child's Fiction," *Canadian Literature*, No. 84 (Spring 1980), pp. 41–56.

14 Louis Vaczek was born in Hungary and spent much of his childhood in Montreal; he graduated from McGill University and served in the RCAF before immigrating to the United States. See *Contemporary Authors*, Clare D. Kinsman and Mary Ann Tennenhouse, eds., vols. 9–12, first revision (Detroit: Gale Research, 1974), pp. 914–15.

[15] See O. J. E. Lunn, "Denys De Saint-Simon, Paul (1649–1731)," *Dictionary of Canadian Biography*, II (Toronto: Univ. of Toronto Press, 1969).

[16] The material in this chapter gives a sense of a genre groping its way toward a more satisfactory way to express its themes. Child's novel occupies a ground that confirms and expands many of the traditional limits found in historical fiction. This is also true of Vaczek's, though in his work the tensions become contradictions rather than polarities. Child's novel is a modernist work with a romantic core; Vaczek's moves along a modernist path only to veer abruptly and follow a more traditional one. The unhaunted, non-symbolic landscape Paul sees is a model of integration and reassurance. Conflicting styles of life are reconciled through a device similar to a camping trip. If there is something like a Canadian dream, it works along those lines. It produces visual replicas of a mystic wilderness that appeal to an audience that must pass its working life in the technological environment. The audience must acquire primitivist perspectives while gazing at them from its cottage verandah or from within a metropolitan art gallery. As refreshing to body and spirit as such activities may prove, they do not penetrate to the core of the dilemma that is posed. The cultural act of imposing so hospitable and humane a structure upon so mute and indifferent an environment does not really solve the estrangement it springs from.

Canada's historical novels parallel our culture's attempt to accomodate itself to modernity. On one side: idealistic reassurances of unending progress and material gain. On the other side: a fictional discourse that acknowledges the shortcomings of those reassurances. Its themes darken and its resolutions grow troubled.

BIBLIOGRAPHY

"Abbot, Johnston" (Edward Montague Ashworth). *La Roux*. New York: Macmillan, 1924.

——. *The Seigneurs of la Soulage: Gentlemen Adventurers of New France two centuries ago*. Toronto: Macmillan, 1928.

Alloway, Mrs. Clement (Mary W.) *Crossed Swords. A Canadian–American Tale of Love and Valor*. Toronto: William Briggs, 1912.

Bennett, Ethel Mary Granger. *Land for Their Inheritance*. Toronto: Ryerson Press, 1955.

——. *Short of the Glory*. Toronto: Ryerson Press, 1960.

——. *A Straw in the Wind*. Toronto: Ryerson Press, 1958.

Benoit, Pierre. *Le marchand de la Place Royale*. Montréal: Fides, 1960.

——. *Martine Juillet, fille du roi*. Montréal: Fides, 1945.

Bird, Will R. *Despite the Distance*. Toronto: Ryerson Press, 1961.

——. *Here Stays Good Yorkshire*. Toronto: Ryerson Press, 1945.

———. *The Passionate Pilgrim*. Toronto: Ryerson Press, 1949.

———. *To Love and To Cherish*. Toronto: Ryerson Press, 1953.

———. *Tristram's Salvation*. New York: Thomas Bouregy, 1957.

Campbell, Grace. *The Higher Hill*. Toronto: Collins, 1944.

———. *Thorn–Apple Tree*. Toronto: Collins, 1942.

Child, Philip. *The Village of Souls*. London: Thornton Butterworth, 1933 and Toronto: Ryerson Press, 1948.

Choquet, Joseph P. *Under Canadian Skies: A French–Canadian Historical Romance*. Providence, Rhode Island: The Oxford Press, 1922.

Clarke, George Frederick. *Return to Acadia*, etc. Fredericton: Brunswick Press, 1952.

"Conan, Laure" (Félicité Angers). *A l'oeuvre et à l'épreuve*. Montréal: Librairie Beauchemin, 1953. Translated into English by Theresa A. Gethin as *The Master–Motive: A Tale of the Days of Champlain*. St. Louis, Mo.: B. Herder, 1909.

———. *L'oublié*. Montréal: Librairie Beauchemin, 1951.

———. *La sève immortelle*. Montréal: Éditions Beauchemin, 1943.

"Connor, Ralph" (Charles William Gordon). *The Rebel Loyalist*. Toronto: McClelland and Stewart, 1935.

———. *The Runner*. Toronto: Doubleday, Doran & Gundy, 1929.

Costain, Thomas B. *High Towers*. Toronto: McClelland and Stewart, 1949.

Cunningham, Louis Arthur. *The King's Fool: A Fascinating Novel of Love Adventure and Intrigue in the Time of Louis xv*. Ottawa: Graphic Publishers, 1931.

Davis, A. R. *The Old Loyalist. A Story of U.E.L. Descendants in Canada*. Toronto: William Briggs, 1908.

Desrosiers, Léo–Paul. *Les engagés du grand portage*. Montréal: Fides, 1980. Présentation et jugements critiques de Maurice Lemire. translated into English by Christina van Oordt as *The Making of Nicolas Montour*. Montreal: Harvest House, 1978.

———. *Nord–sud*. Montréal: Fides, 1980. Présentation et jugements critiques de Maurice Lemire.

———. *Les opinâtres*. Montréal: Fides, 1954. Préparé de Jean–Noel Tremblay.

Dunham, Mabel. *Toward Sodom*. Toronto: Macmillan, 1927.

———. *The Trail of the Conestoga*. Toronto: McClelland and Stewart, 1942.

———. *The Trail of the King's Men*. Toronto: Ryerson Press, [1931].

Eaton, Evelyn. *Quietly My Captain Waits*. New York: Literary Guild, 1940.

———. *Restless Are the Sails*. New York: Harper & Bros., 1941.

———. *The Sea Is So Wide*. New York: Harper & Bros., 1943.

Elson, John *The Scarlet Sash. A Romance of the Old Niagara Frontier*. Toronto: Dent, 1925.

Fraser, A. Ermatinger. *The Drum of Lanoraye*, etc. Toronto: Ryerson Press, [1932].

French, Maida Parlow. *All This to Keep*. Toronto: Collins, 1947.

———. *Boughs Bend Over*. Toronto: McClelland and Stewart, 1943.

Grahame, Gordon Hill. *The Bond Triumphant*. Toronto: Hodder & Stoughton, 1923.

Hodgson, John C. J. *Lion and Lily, a Story of New France*. Montréal: Renouf, 1935.

Laurent, Albert. *L'épopée tragique: Roman Acadien*. Montréal: Éditions Beauchemin, 1956.

Lighthall, W. D. *The Master of Life: A Romance of the Five Nations of Prehistoric Montreal*. Toronto; Musson, 1908.

MacGillivray, Carrie Holmes. *The Shadow of Tradition*. Ottawa: Graphic Publishers, [1927].

McDowell, Franklin Davey. *The Champlain Road*. Toronto: Macmillan, 1939.

Morisset, Gérard. *Novembre 1775: Nouvelle*. Québec: n.p., 1948.

Niven, Frederick. *The Flying Years*. London: Collins, 1935.

——. *Mine Inheritance*. London: Collins, 1940.

——. *The Transplanted*. Toronto: Collins, 1944.

"North, Anison" (May Wilson). *The Forging of the Pikes. A Romance of the Upper Canadian Rebellion of 1837*. New York: George H. Doran, 1920.

O'Hagan, Howard. *Tay John*. Toronto: McClelland and Stewart, 1974.

"Price–Brown" (Eric Bohn). *In the Van. "The Builders."* Toronto: McLeod & Allen, 1906.

——. *Laura the Undaunted*. Toronto: Ryerson Press, 1930.

——. *The Mac's of '37: A Story of the Canadian Rebellion*. Toronto: McLeod & Allen, 1910.

Raddall, Thomas. *The Governor's Lady*. New York: Doubleday, 1960.

——. *Hangman's Beach*. New York: Doubleday, 1966.

——. *His Majesty's Yankees*. Toronto: McClelland and Stewart, 1977.

——. *Pride's Fancy*. Toronto: McClelland and Stewart, 1974 [1946].

——. *Rogert Sudden*. Toronto: McClelland and Stewart, 1972 [1944].

Roquebrune, Robert Laroque de. *D'un océan à l'autre*. Paris: Éditions du monde nouveau, 1924.

——. *Les habits rouges*. Montréal: Fides, 1978.

"Roylat, Jane" (Jean Taylor). *The Lily of Fort Garry*. Toronto: Dent, 1930.

——. *Wilderness Walls*. Toronto: Dent, 1933.

Sellar, Robert. *Hemlock, a Tale of the War of 1812 and Gleaner Tales*. Huntingdon, Québec: Gleaner Bookroom, 1918.

——. *Morven*. Huntingdon, Québec: Gleaner Bookroom, 1911.

Servos, Launcelot Cressy. *Frontenac and the Maid of the Mist*. Toronto: Hal DeGruchy Co., 1927.

Stead, Robert J. C. *The Homesteaders*. Toronto: Univ. of Toronto Press, 1973.

Sullivan, Alan. *The Fur Masters*. New York: Coward–McCann, 1947.

——. *The Great Divide*. London: Lovat Dickson & Thompson, 1935.

——. *Three Came to Ville Marie*. Toronto: Oxford Univ. Press, 1941.

Teskey, Adeline M. *Candlelight Days*. London: Cassell, 1913.

Thil–Lorrain, Michel. *Nélida ou les guerres Canadiennes* 1812–1814. Paris: Editions Casterman, [1912].

Vaczek, Louis. *River and Empty Sea*. Boston: Houghton Mifflin, 1950.

Three

THE APPEARANCE of Anne Hébert's *Kamouraska* in 1970 began a rebirth of the historical novel in Canada; the genre was beginning to attract our finest literary imaginations. The historical novel can no longer be viewed as the preserve of inferior talents. Alterations began to appear in the genre as writers began to handle historical material in new and complex ways. This chapter discusses four superior Canadian novels: Hébert's *Kamouraska*, Rudy Wiebe's *The Temptations of Big Bear* (1973), Timothy Findley's *The Wars* (1977) and Graeme Gibson's *Perpetual Motion* (1982). As well, we look at a number of other works that indicate changes in the genre.

I

Critics of *Kamouraska* have concentrated on its Gothicism and its fairy-tale elements: the book has not been examined as historical fiction.[1] After all, historical fiction has attracted scant and perfunctory attention from scholars and critics in this country. Also, the Gothic aspects of the novel remain its most attention-getting features, even as listing them forms the staple of discussion about the other fiction of Anne Hébert.[2] This Gothicism permeates all her fiction: it may have a distinct historical setting as in *Kamouraska*, a recent one as in *Les enfants du sabbat* (1975) or *Les fous de Bassan* (1982), or even an up-to-date location (*Héloïse*, 1980). The fact that the actual story happened in the past offers no explanation as to why the author kept it there. The fictional possibilities of the eternal triangle are limitless; its affinities with Gothicism are ineradicable; no particular setting lords it over the others in the matter of exploiting the possibilities of such material.

Yet Hébert chose to write the book in the historical mode. It seems safe to assume that Hébert, a serious author, would not choose a setting frivolously. She accumulated a mass of detail to present a convincing (not necessarily realistic) sense of the past, and the book gives the reader the sense of another time.

What Hébert's novel says about its subject and setting at first seems secondary to the novel's plot, for the impact of events in this tale of "la violence, le sang et la neige" focusses the reader's attention. Readers are tempted to respond to the novel as if they were its mad narrator. Elisabeth d'Aulnières Tassy Rolland views herself as a *loup garou*, or zombie ("Dans un champ aride, sous les pierres, on a déterré une femme noire, vivante, datant d'une époque reculée et sauvage. Étrangement conservée.") But she is more than that.

In a prefatory note, the author states that she has retained only "leurs gestes les plus extérieurs, les plus officiels" from historical figures; the rest "sont devenus mes créatures imaginaires, au cours d'un lent cheminement intérieur." Hébert has fashioned them to an end.

Elisabeth wanders among three worlds. The genteel world into which she was born, the world of her mother and her hovering aunts, is graceful and passive. They're French; they get along well with their English overlords. The first man she marries, Antoine Tassy, Sieur de Kamouraska, belongs to the second world, to a seigneurial class in decline. He is comfortable among the common people. Although she is repelled by his brutality, Elisabeth is attracted to his vitality. The two first met on a duck hunt. (Her aunts did not want her to attend.) Couched in the duck blind with Tassy, Elisabeth feels the pull of his sexuality. "Et cela me plairait aussi d'être sous lui, me débattant, tandis qu'il m'embrasserait le visage avec de gross basiers mouillés."

The third world, the world of high, death-seeking passion exemplified by Doctor George Nelson, forms a fiction within the fiction. Nelson appears first as Tassy's old classmate, then as Elisabeth's lover and finally as Tassy's murderer. Yet he is never a solid presence in the story; he is partly a creation of Elisabeth's fantasy life, which Hébert depicts with terrifying brilliance. Elisabeth and Nelson are genteel adulterers who long for respectability. They use the sluttish servant girl, Aurélie Caron, a low, realistic parody of her mistress's high-flown passion. Unsatisfied with using her as a go-between, they try to make a killer of her: they dress her in Elisabeth's clothes and try to mesmerize her into killing. Elisabeth and Nelson are less in love with each other than with the fantasy they have created. This fantasy lives behind their reckless, theatrical display of nudity at the windows of an isolated cabin.

Finally Tassy is murdered. Nelson parades a blood-stained sleigh and harness before every inn-keeper on the road, indicating how little planning went into the wretched business. Yet it is this world Elisabeth says she longs for, a world of undying passion and passionate death:

> Tout comme si le meurte d'Antoine n'était pour nous que le pro-longement suprémè de l'amour.
> Nous ferions sans doute aussi bien de nous tuer, tous les deux ensemble . . . . Avant que la vie quotidienne n'altère notre pure fureur de vivre et de mourir.

The novel's significance as psychological and historical fiction lies in its narrative frame. The reader first encounters Elisabeth as Elisabeth d'Aulnières Tassy Rolland, eighteen years a faithful wife to a solicitor, who is now dying. Before his heart weakened. Jérôme Rolland insisted on his conjugal rights nearly every night. He gave Elisabeth eight children; she had two by Tassy and one by George Nelson. Rolland may prudently display a certain apprehensiveness when Elisabeth gives him his medicine, but eighteen years can dull public memory. Mme Rolland of the Rue du Parloir, one of the walking dead, moves in respectable company. (Nelson fled to the United States when the law went after him.)

We have, in effect, two novels. One is the *Kamouraska* of the critics: the *grand guignol* of black horses and sleighs streaking across a snow-bound landscape flecked with blood. Here are the echoes of Quebec folk-legends, of *loups-garoux* and pacts with Satan.[3] Here is the madwoman obsessed with mirrors, windows and confinement. This is the stuff of superb enter-tainment, with its images of terror and destruction. Yet there is another *Kamouraska*, the chronicle of a cold bourgeoise who has endured eleven confinements, but in childbed rather than in prison. Here is the romantic woman who built a Satanic façade around a sordid *crime passionel* and sought to garb a whorish servant girl in the robes of Hell. Here is the bold killer who scuttled across the border to safety and the lawless woman who managed to marry well once more. The novel is full of Gothicism and irony and oscillates between melodrama and farce.

What does this have to do with history? Imagine that Elisabeth is the petit bourgeois Quebec, stifled in respectability, relieved that 1837 is past, obsessed by fantasies, torn between passive respectability and anarchy. She is a Quebec locked firmly in the embrace of the Church and of those three aunts (Tassy called them nuns) who will perjure themselves to save their niece's good name. There is another Quebec, the brawling, whoring, booz-ing rural life Tassy represents. Yet for all its potency, Tassy's Quebec is ultimately distasteful. Tassy cannot be romanticized into an earthy, vital seigneur; his brutality and callousness cannot be overlooked. Where, then, is the gift of life to be found? A semblance of life appears in the guise of

56

Nelson, the "Anglo." He is not a typical American — his parents were Loyalists who remained in the United States after the Revolution. Like Tassy, Nelson was educated in the classical system. He was formed by both the United States and English Canada. Nelson, a country doctor in Quebec, takes an innovative, scientific approach to medicine; he disdains the traditional practices of his colleagues. He is more modern and rational than any of the French Canadians in the novel. Yet when things fall apart, he proves to be an unreliable partner. He commits the murder ineptly, then realizes that safety is a better fate than melodramatic acceptance of destiny. He repudiates his partner in the rhetoric of bewildered innocence and *in English*: "*It is that damned woman that has ruined me.*" (emphasis in original)[4]

The respectable, accommodating Quebec we see on the surface is wracked by unattainable and ultimately self-destructive fantasies — madness. Madness stalks the other novels of Anne Hébert and forms much of the action in the fiction of Marie-Claire Blais; there is madness in Hubert Aquin's *Prochain épisode* (1965) and Jacques Godbout's *Le couteau sur la table* (1965).

Kamouraska is not a fully articulated nationalist allegory, but the novel works beyond the level of a psycho-thriller set for no reason in the past, and it delivers a disturbing, lurid vision of a Quebec in crisis.

Kamouraska began a new phase in the writing of Canadian historical fiction: imaginative readers saw that material that could have been served up as a Gothicized romance was also amenable to the powers of a serious writer.

II

Beautiful Losers, a novel dealing with the flotsam of contemporary experience, incorporates into its mosaic bits and pieces from the past. Like many novels, including *The Village of Souls*, Cohen's novel owed some of its incidents to the *Jesuit Relations*. *Beautiful Losers* was widely read and reviewed, and thus signalled the arrival of the post-modernist sensibility in Canadian fiction.

The novel does not deal with history *per se*, but it does fabricate a myth about Canadian history. In the novel, the rule of reason and repression that has marked the old era must give way to the powers of magic and exuberance. Cohen's broken losers — especially the demented F. — fight against order, reason and the strict control of sexuality. The novelist found the origins of this bondage in the life of one of the first Canadian saints,

Kateri Tekakwitha, the Lily of the Mohawks. Her denial of fleshly appetite and her ascetic death (recounted from the *Relations*) serve as extremes against which moderns can measure their own conduct. Tekakwitha springs out of sacred history into the pop mythology of the novel. But the mythology is far from reassuring: Tekakwitha despises the flesh and is destroyed. Edith, the passive, put-upon heroine, revels in the flesh; she also is destroyed. The moral offers no comfort. The novel is important here because it indicates a shift in the cultural climate: historical material became a popular and accessible fuel for the writer's inspiration. To construct a demanding, inaccessible literature was no longer a requirement for any writer laying a claim to seriousness. Cohen's novel used many of the features of literary modernism — the emphasis on sexuality, the use of non-linear narrative form, the relegation of the moralistic past to the trash heap — and added something new: the acceptance of the homogenized, synthetically created mass culture that had been modernism's despised foe. The new element stood out like a wax banana in a still life of real oranges. In *Beautiful Losers*, history and the playful exploitation of it become fun. The historical novel, with its seriousness and its search for significant visions of our culture, was accompanied by a kind of fiction that embraced historical material as part of the playground fiction was free to gambol in. History's solemnities were shaken into new patterns, which signified the finding of absurdity rather than the search for meaning. We shall look at a few examples of this new spirit.

Two novels dealing with the theme of cross-cultural confusion as seen in the early years of New France are David Kevan's *Racing Tides* (1982) and Brian Moore's *Black Robe* (1985). The first begins at the beginning, with Champlain's settlement of Port Royal in 1605. Humorous and ironic in tone, the narrative of Sodric du Gaelle passes bewilderedly through his immersion into the confusions of "American" life. The "science" of the colonizers bears as heavy a load of bias and superstition as the mythology of the primitives. As if in promise of a sequel, the novel concludes with a cipher. Let that puzzle be an emblem for the entire tale, as white and red cultures cannot help but stump each other.

New France in the 1640s provides Moore's setting, as the Jesuit missionary Laforgue strains to make sense of a bizarre reality no European culture could have prepared him for. The novel's relative vagueness about space and time, the confusion of the central character, elicit a response similar to that of *The Village of Souls*. The mutual bafflement between Black-robes and Savages is the novel's central motif. Christian dogma provides an analogue to Huron animism. Laforgue by the end of the novel has endured a series of horrific, unassimilable experiences leading him to question the value of his evangelizing mission. He continues his killing labours because he has come to love his Savages, however much his Christianity keeps him from understanding them

The *Oxford Companion* classifies Jacques Ferron's *Le ciel de Québec* (1969) as a historical novel.[5] Ferron (1921–1985) uses history without writing it. Precise in its dating, his novel describes life in Quebec in 1937 and 1938. Real, even famous people appear in the book: Monsignor Camille Roy, Cardinal Villeneuve, Maurice Duplessis, Hector de Saint-Denys-Garneau, Anne Hébert, F.R.Scott, Paul-Émile Borduas. They are figures in a puppet show. Crazy things happen to them. They go to Purgatory or to the Canadian west. Their identities are assumed by mythological doubles. Their dreams are greater than reality. Their lives are compressed or speeded up according to the demands of the narrative. The novel pays scant attention to the demands of actual space and time.

Le ciel de Québec appeared a year before *Kamouraska*. The two novels are very different. The narrative of *Kamouraska* follows "interior" drives and logic, yet Hébert keeps those events interiorized. Elisabeth never becomes the monster she sees herself as: her real life is too prosaic for that. She and Nelson may think of themselves in operatic–mythological terms, but they are just two people, nothing more. *Kamouraska*'s message must be elucidated.

Any reader who puts Ferron's novel down and misses the message has not understood the book. His work is a satire. It presents a group of characters who are viewed not as individuals but as containers for ideas and attitudes. Ferron has a target; all his characters are circles on that target. Loosely speaking, his target is the "anywhere but here" attitude toward Quebec life and culture. For example, literary mandarins who seek to express themselves in an internationalist, modernist mode weaken Quebec culture. The Church, with its eyes fixed on an outmoded agrarian, hierarchical model of society, weakens the culture. Westmount Anglophones who want to change Quebec without shedding their linguistic and social defenses weaken the culture. Figures like St.-Denys-Garneau, an artistic model to English Canadians, and Anne Hébert, who took lengthy sojourns in France and criticized Quebec, are mercilessly mauled. Ferron's satire has a greater polemic thrust to it than Cohen's. Parts of it work like a *roman à clef*. Yet both works follow a classical model: they attack the cultural stance of persons whose individuality is of less importance than their fictional character. Fictional history is presented in a form different from its traditional guise. The climate for innovation heats up.

Evidence of this innovation is found in what might be called "historical romps." Donald Jack's Bandy series (1962–   ), Richard B. Wright's *Farthing's Fortunes* (1976) and Heather Robertson's projected series on "The King Years" (1983–   ) present new material for consideration. None of these novels displays the grand manner. They do not strive to elucidate history, only to display its absurdity. They do not feature tightly knit plots or characters of large and introspective souls. Instead, people who more or less know what they are doing glide through picaresque plots.

Donald Jack (1921–) wrote the light-hearted Bandy series: *Three Cheers for Me* (1962), *That's Me in the Middle* (1973), *It's Me Again* (two parts, 1975), *Me Bandy, You Cissie* (1979) and *Me Too* (1983). The roguish hero is dragged through scrape after scrape during the Great War and after. The perpetually naïve, obtuse yet resourceful Bandy meets the famous folk of the time. Bandy's adventures combine the stock formulas of popular comic fiction (feckless hero swept up in military bureaucracy; sexual escapades and misadventures; hints of new adventures to come), but they do not attain the level of high farce. They remain good entertainments.

The first of Robertson's projected series, *Willie. A Romance*, includes careful characterization, density of detail and great imagination in plotting. The fictional W. L. M. King appears no more buffoonish than the real one portrayed in C. P. Stacey's *A Very Double Life* (1976). Robertson surrounds him with a large cast from the Ottawa of his time. As well, she creates in her narrator an engaging, common-sense figure who serves as a filter of events. The author's command of historical material allows her to mix its elements in adventurous ways; thus the heroic, doomed Talbot Papineau serves as a foil to the beaverish, self-important King.

Richard Wright's novel *Farthing's Fortunes* is propelled by a rambling, picaresque plot and is crammed with bizarre coincidence and outrageous characters. At first it appears to be a rollicking farce. Wright is skillful when he creates Billy Farthing, his slow-witted narrator, and a light-hearted gloss coats what is a very sombre scene. In this Canadian *Candide*, Billy wanders Canada, the United States and the Sommme during the Great War in search of the elusive, idealized, sluttish Sally Butters. Billy is bumpkinish and unreflective; Sally is street-wise. Over the years, Billy is fleeced by nearly everyone. He delivers an authoritative summation:

> To be dragged out and kicked and humbled by your fellow man
> is a grievous loss to your dignity . . . . if you were down on your
> luck you had to depend on the charity of your fellow man. And
> I always found that about as thin as boarding house soup.

Billy's bitter knowledge contrasts with the unsinkable optimism of the American con man, Findlater, to whom Billy attaches himself at various times. Findlater's schemes become grubbier and grubbier. In Billy's last glimpse of him, the obese Findlater squats in a decayed mansion in a Florida swamp while the aged, skeletal Sally seeks to perpetuate the good old days of her success as a vaudeville chanteuse. At this point, Billy's story concludes and the framing device of the prissy editor who discovered the narrator in a senior-citizens' home concludes the novel.

When we stop laughing, we are left with the image of a greedy Canadian bumpkin whose crooked naïvety is exploited easily by the slicker and more calloused American trickster. The book depicts the Canadian's jackal-like willingness to be led. The novel's message might be about our complicity in the United States enterprise in Vietnam; it might be a satire on a common colonial attitude toward the schemes of our Big Neighbour. No one could ignore the disgust that permeates the book.

Farthing's Fortunes belongs on any list of historical novels. Its thematic and narrative links with Voltaire's satire and its moralistic message tie this work to other satires I have discussed. Wright employs history as a backdrop for zany events, as did Donald Jack and Heather Robertson. Wright does not focus upon a single historical event; instead, he drags a puppet across the stage of history and grants him long life so he may tell of the Klondike, The Great War, the Depression and so on. The novel deals with an amalgam of historical events in a reasonably detailed and convincing fashion. It attempts to give the hero's adventures some sense of greater significance, albeit a gloomy one. The other works examined in this chapter range from full-fledged historical fiction — *Kamouraska* — to satires that use historical material — *Beautiful Losers* and *Le ciel de Québec* — to light-hearted farces — the Bandy series and *Willie. Farthing's Fortunes* is a hybrid that uses all these elements.

III

While these alternative versions of historical fiction were being written, the traditional modes of expression had not disappeared. One example is a series, "Les fils de la liberté," by Louis Caron (1942–   ). Two volumes — *Le canard de bois* (1981) and *La corne de brume* (1982) — have appeared so far. An earlier novel, *L'emmitouflé*, was published in 1977. The hero of the earlier novel, an American of French-Canadian ancestry, flees to Quebec to avoid being drafted and sent to Vietnam. In Québec, he learns of an uncle who evaded Canadian conscription during the First World War. The uncle's hideaway is set in the region of Nicolet, where most of the action in the historical series takes place.

Le canard de bois deals with 1837 and its aftermath and with 1935. In 1837, Hyacinthe Bellerose struggles, is defeated and is sent into exile; in 1935, his descendant Bruno emerges into young manhood and the beginnings of reconciliation with his ancestry. In the ballot-box, legislative-assembly sense of the term, politics does not occupy the volumes, yet both books are concerned with the struggle of competing groups to hold or attain power. The first book deals with the exploitation of a man oppressed by a system that offers him a glimpse of false freedom. As the novel begins, Hyacinthe is a defeated man: he is returning from an ill-fated attempt at colonization accompanied by the corpse of his wife and by an orphan boy of Irish ancestry whom he has chosen to care for. Home in Port St. François, he shocks the villagers when he takes up with a Métis Christian, Marie-Moitié. Papineau's follower in the village, one Major Hubert, incites the populace to rebel. The rebels are defeated, and in the ensuing confusion they try to find a cache of arms from the United States. Hyacinthe tries to talk the villagers out of their doomed enterprise; he fails. The villagers barricade themselves in a church. The English soldiers easily rout them, and Hyacinthe is exiled. The orphan, Tim, adopts the name Bellerose; he is the hero in *La corne de brume*. As the first part of the book ends, Tim and Marie-Moitié watch Hyacinthe's prison-ship sail away. In 1935, Bruno is setting out for the larger world after spending time in a logging camp. A wooden duck carved by Hyacinthe serves as a token that connects the generations.

The novel presents a leftist nationalist viewpoint. The scorn for the bourgeois revolution planned by Papineau is as intense in Caron's work as in Claire De Lamirande's *Papineau ou l'épée à double tranchant* (1980), for example. That book presents a series of interior monologues in which Papineau's failings and betrayals haunt him. The injustices in Caron's book stem from the class system rather than from ethnic considerations; the forces of evil cross ethnic lines. A brutal merchant may be an *anglais*, but so is a benign seigneur. The notary Plessis and Major Hubert may be Franco-phone, but they are attempting to gain a place at the top by inciting the workers to violence. The village priest may dislike the Protestant English, but their regime buttresses his Church. Hyacinthe's Irish orphan is despised, but the villagers do not understand that he also is a victim of the bosses. Hyacinthe may be a hero, but the author is careful to keep him a working-class hero.

The book's ideology is similar to populism or romantic Marxism, where class lines prove stronger than ethnicity or religion in determining an individual's fate and allegiances. As well, the vision of refinement–through–suffering that powered so much of the French-Canadian fiction discussed in the opening chapter is found here also. *Les Acadiens nouveaux* are set apart from the impure according to the norms of a materialist ideology rather than a Christian–romantic one. An itinerant tinker concludes that Hyacinthe is one of those who are "designes pour porter la misère des autres." This reminds us that, while ideologies may change, images abide.

The politics in the second novel seem less doctrinaire. Tim Bellerose is a flawed character. Flagrantly unfaithful to his wife, hot-tempered, impulsive and not totally honest, he constantly struggles against his fate. Temporary successes are followed by disaster as Tim tries to run his own shipping business. (This motif recalls Jacques Ferron's *Le Saint-Elias* [1972], in which the building and launching of a trading vessel serves as French Canada's window on the world.) Tim's impulsiveness helps to do him in; he is also undone by the North West Rebellion and the hanging of Riel. Desperate and frustrated, he jumps into the river, holding a copper foghorn — a device used by the author to link the stories. Bruno still has the carved duck, but he leaves home.

The epigraphs to each chapter are taken from Félix-Antoine Savard's *Menaud, maître–draveur* (1937), a political fable masquerading (inadequately) as a novel; they prove a tip-off. The work's ceaseless chant that "les étrangères" are stealing Quebec predicts the ideology of Caron's work. Not all "strangers" in the book prove offensive: a Jewish money-lender who supports Tim emerges as the cleanest businessman in the novel. And Tim's character is itself complex. Tim delivers the message that French Canadians cannot expect success until they are self-reliant: they will never be "chez-eux dans ce pays que le jour ou les machines à vapeur . . . porterent leur nom en lettres de cuivre sur leurs flancs. Pas avant." Tim's downfall stems from his fierce ambition; he scorns French Canadians for lacking ambition. Without a culture to mediate and support his drives, those drives become self-destructive. Tim dies bankrupt, an outcast. The clear-cut ideology complements the simple characterizations and story lines, providing easily digestible material. The series is proof that the historical novel as nationalist statement remains a living tradition in French Canada.

The same could be said for English Canada, where the nationalist ideology is inclusionist rather than exclusionist. Robert Wall (1937–   ) began a series called *The Canadians*, which offers four volumes to date: *Blackrobe* (1981), *Bloodbrothers* (1981), *Birthright* (1982) and *Patriots* (1983). Like a soap opera in its convolutions, the series traces an extended family and its history in this country since its beginnings. The series shows a profound allegiance to the era of multiculturalism. The characters include Jesuits, fur traders, citizens of New France, Indians, Americans, Loyalists, French Canadians and so on. The novels strive to amalgamate all these characters into One Big Canada. In contrast to Caron's series, which deals with endurance, defeat, frustration and the recognition of painful limits, Wall's series moves its characters through struggle after struggle and gives those struggles an optimistic resolution. More than two hundred years have passed since the fall of Quebec; these two series appear to confirm each culture in a familiar mood, the one of confinement, the other of assimilation.

The series indicate the climate of acceptance and interest in which historical fiction is now produced. One of the reasons for the current high quality of Canadian historical novels is that they are written by superior novelists who adopt the historical genre as they might any other in the course of their artistic development. Hugh MacLennan's *Voices in Time* (1980) and Hugh Hood's *New Age* series (1975–   ) show that playing with past and future time has become one of our novelists' chief pastimes. The fiction of past time, then, is not "there" in some dessicated, archival fashion, but as a lively form of fictional expression.

IV

Timothy Findley's choice of the Great War as material for his third novel was scarcely a ground-breaking one. When he chose the subject — or it chose him[6] — the risk lay not in mapping new territory, but in exploiting ground that had been occupied by so many others, writers from many countries.[7] Findley chose an archival narrative framework for the book.[8] The device embodies a sense of the "pastness" of the material. Findley's fiction relies on imagination rather than memory. As well, Findley acknowledges the narrator's non-participatory status, indicating that the story's events are set in a remote historical past.

The gesture also warns the audience that, in the style of post-modern "metafiction," it is the conventions of story-telling that are under examination. Those conventions have become the objects of artistic play. The narrator was never "there." He can only reconstruct "there" from the fragments left behind by participants. We remain in his hands. The book announces that Robert Ross "didn't think it consciously" and that "his body hadn't waited for his mind. It did things on its own." We realize that, for the events in the novel, "There is no good picture of this except the one you can make in your mind." History is being turned into fiction. Critics will decide how authentic the fiction is; historians will judge the authenticity of the history.[9] As in *Kamouraska*, we are plunged into an examination of interior states. Yet we are also exposed to events and processes that have undergone extensive historical treatment. A widespread assumption is given credence: implicit in every historical novel is an examination of present concerns couched in the presentation of past events. We know that the events of the world wars are past for us, and must also have been in the author's past, so we assume that we are reading historical fiction. But the "history" is the writer's actual past. Findley's novel is not about the Great War and modern memory, but about the great past and the imaginative reconstruction of it. Findley's narrative voice is the anonymous archival burrower, and so the author can display the tools of the imaginative archaeologist.

Of course, it is not a "real" past the archivist is uncovering; the work is fiction. But I would like to examine the statements the novel makes about history, particularly our history. The Great War is a central experience in the nation's history. Findley does not present any sustained message about the war. Historians debate how Canada's casualties and the energy and resources the country gave to the war effort affected Canadian nationalism. A traditional historical novel might offer a meditation on this subject. A young Canadian, for example, might discover his new-worldliness when thrown into the chaos of the old, or he might experience the conflict as a distraction from the process of nation-building. Such possibilities are remote from *The Wars*. Traditional nationalist concerns describe a reality that lies between the personal and the cosmic. No such middle ground exists in Findley's novel. Robert Ross fights two personal wars. One is on this side of the ocean, against his family: its stuffiness, repression and deathliness. The death of his sister, the killing of her pets, the alcoholism and sexual hysteria of his mother and the impotent remoteness of his father are left behind when Ross boards the troopship. Over the water lies the other war, a hideous, gigantic, institutionalized embodiment of Ross's deadly inner forces.

Ross seeks to skirt the death and madness of both wars. He loses because of his inability to protect non-human victims — his sister's rabbits at home and the horses in Europe. His burning and disfigurement are prefigured in the casualties he encounters throughout the novel. They are outward signs of the inward maimings he undergoes.

When Ross tries to rescue the horses, the military recaptures the animals. It is only one of the humiliations Ross endures. He discovers his own fears when he shoots a harmless enemy soldier; he discovers his inability to withstand assaults on his person when he is raped in a bath-house; he struggles in vain against what everyone else accepts as routine. Only a photograph remains of happier days, a picture of Robert and Rowena alive and well.

We move from this personal experience to a cosmic dimension of destiny and natural order. Ross's gravestone is inscribed with a list of the four elements, earth, air, fire and water. The novel excludes the no-man's-land of politics, war and nationalism. A sense of selfhood, a sense of how this selfhood fits into the larger order: the novel is mute on any solution to these issues.

The novel seems to have nothing to do with any national vision, so it is unique in Canadian historical fiction. The middle ground of politics and society is a killing ground. One critic has written that the film version of the novel "vividly evokes the colonial world at the moment of its slipping into the maelstrom of World War I."[10] The novel does this only to illustrate how destructive that colonial experience is to any humane enterprise. In the novel, home front and battlefield blend. There are humane presences in the book — comrades, lovers, animals — the rest is death.

The novel also plays with the conventions of fiction writing and history. Findley does not discuss the war years as they have generally been discussed in our culture; he does not locate, in the war, evidence for national advance or for national disintegration. Whatever life remains is contained in snapshots, tapes, and reminiscences. The book concludes with a photo of Robert and his sister in a peaceful moment before the war, which has, scrawled on its back, "'Look! You can see our breath!'" "And you can," the narrator adds laconically. What you see is all you have.

The Wars presents new departures in technique and theme. *Kamouraska* interiorized the historical novel: its traditional material was handled as psychological fiction yet contained a complex vision. *The Wars* demonstrates that the historical novel can be post-modern. The archive serves as a narrative device; its symbolism is pointed. It is appropriate to the novel's meaning and to its mode of story-telling. By their nature, archives are fragmentary and subject to interpretation; the novel's events are also fragmentary and open to interpretation. The novel also contains a thematic innovation: the traditional historical novel reinforced the concept of Canadian nationalism. Findley's novel instead presents a vision of life in which nationalism is not central; it distracts the hero from his attempt to find his place in the universe. History can no longer force the novelist in a defined and well-worn direction; instead, it can be shaped by the craftsman's hand.

V

The malleability of material also marks Graeme Gibson's *Perpetual Motion*. Gibson's technique is more traditional than Findley's; in *Perpetual Motion*, tradition and innovation are combined to create a superior work of fiction.

A passage from the writing of George Grant offers a restatement of Gibson's theme:

> When one contemplates the conquest of nature by technology one must remember that the conquest had to include our own bodies. Calvinism provided the determined and organized men and women who could rule the mastered world. The punishment they inflicted on non-human nature, they had first inflicted on themselves.

Now when from that primal [encounter with the New World environment on the part of European newcomers] has come forth what is present before us; when the victory over the land leaves most of us in metropoloi where widely spread consumption vies with confusion and squalor . . . one must remember now the hope, the stringency and nobility of that primal encounter . . . . Whatever the vulgarity of mass industrialism, however empty our talk of democracy, it must not be forgotten that in the primal there was the expectation of a new independence in which each would be free for self-legislation, and for communal legislation . . . . To know that parents had to force the instincts of their children to the service of pioneering control . . . must not be to forget what was necessary and heroic in that conquest.[11]

The grandeurs and miseries of that primal encounter are captured in Gibson's novel, which at first had a contemporary setting. Gibson said the choice of a bygone time "sort of crept up on me."

Yet he denies that *Perpetual Motion* is a historical novel:

While Perpetual Motion [sic] is set in our past, it isn't a historical novel. That is, I didn't try to present southern Ontario in the 1860s or 1870s as it was, or might have been, in what I understand to be the "historical" sense. I didn't do much objective research, or analysis, and instead of worrying about my bias, I indulged it. As a writer, I was more concerned with internal consistency, the logic of the book itself, than with verifiability, more concerned with invention than with representation.[12]

Yet *Perpetual Motion* is a historical novel. The "internal consistency, the logic of the book itself" and the book's convincing details offer a portrait of a past society that is a meditation on the present. The book marches between the rural idyll and the historical novel. Gibson gives his fiction a dense historical flavour, and the book evokes with care and patience the culture it observes on the verge of a break-up. Certain turns of phrase, fluent expositions of farming and mechanical processes and stories are used to tell the tale of a single man's passage from an agrarian to a technological era. The language of the novel calls attention to itself: "telluric," "banausic," "stridulate," "melismatic," "aphonic" and "eristic" are words Gibson uses to provide "a sound and rhythm that would give the sense of another time and place."[13] The vocabulary underlines the author's ability to convey the rhythms of another time. Traditionally, the historical novel uses present benefits to justify past trials. Gibson's novel reverses that thematic pattern.

The story follows the career of an inept farmer, Robert Fraser. His obsessions and ineptitude cause his mastery of new forms of technological-entrepreneurial enterprise. Fraser gains substantial success. His attempts to create a perpetual-motion machine cause a spectacular smash, but his skills in the factory-hunting of passenger pigeons bring him wealth and position. He buys a new house. He fathers a son, who flees to the wilds, and a daughter, who is single-minded and acquisitive. His wife falls by the wayside.

The story of an obsessive person who bends his life toward the remaking of himself and whose triumph manifests itself in a great house that will stand as a monument is a North American trope. (In refracted form, it looms behind *The Great Gatsby*. It stands as the set of *Mourning Becomes Electra*. Faulkner told the story first as tragedy in *Absalom, Absalom!* and then as farce in *The Mansion*. It forms the subject of Frederick Philip Grove's *Fruits of the Earth* and appears as the theme of Robert J. C. Stead's *The Homesteaders*, until the conventions of melodrama overwhelm the story's coherence.) Gibson adds to this tradition, but his story is more than a moral account. Fraser is driven not merely by greed and the yearning for immortality, but also by boundless curiosity and will, the mark of the technological man. Fraser is a decidedly prosaic Upper Canadian whose most vivid dreams glow with a rational, pragmatic aura.

Often, historical novels that present regional idylls are written in a composed tone; they present a moment captured in time. Jacques Ferron's *Le Saint-Elias* (1972) and Antonine Maillet's *Pélagie-la-charrette* (1979) are two examples. Ferron's book combines themes of a closed-in Quebec's efforts to contact the great world beyond, the resistance of a people to the Church's straitened orthodoxy in sexual matters and the roots of the author's imagination.

More an epical folk ballad than a novel, *Pélagie-la-charrette* follows the story of the Acadien return from exile in the evocation of the unstoppable heroine who gathers all manner of people into her cart. Through anecdote and incident it sings the story of a people and their tenuous survival against enemies within and without. Both works skillfully outline a past whose results are with us still. Such a feeling bears a far greater intensity in *Perpetual Motion*; the book's concern with the role technology plays in society leaps out from the page. As well, Gibson chose for his theme a fact of modernity that will endure as long as our culture does: the theme of change. Most historical novels discuss the theme of accommodation to the New World, and convey a message of reassurance: "The early process is over; we now need to see how we got here." Gibson's subject has no end, because the dreamings of the culture it portrays are limitless. An endless future is implied in a final sentence, which leads nowhere and everywhere: "And thus began a desolate search that would last for the rest of his life because, try as he might — and, Jesus, didn't he do the best he could? — all they ever found was the moon."

"They" are looking for the remnants of the perpetual-motion machine — a huge orrery — that whirled itself apart. But the real moon remains. It is at once the moon of the lunatic and the moon our technology landed on. Perpetual motion may be a chimera, but the search for it involves man in scientific-technological endeavours that amplify his mastery of nature. Our instruments for mimicking the progression of the heavenly bodies — perpetual motion — are more sophisticated than Fraser's, but the search for the moon continues; our culture can never abandon that search. Hence the openness of the ending, the dynamism of the theme and the flawless dovetailing of theme and subject.

The novel contains a set of polarities and recurring associations. One is a set-piece, the great pigeon hunt. The incident takes place after 1876, a very late date in the history of the passenger pigeon. (The last one died in the Cincinnati zoo in 1914.) Shortly before the great hunt, Fraser sees a netted flock of them and thinks they are "survivors . . . life itself." The birds first appear as a gigantic infestation. Fraser understands that the plague can be turned to profit; there is more wealth to be made from selling supplies and transportation to hunters than from selling dead pigeons. In another enterprise, Fraser attempts to corner the green peas in his district, in order to drive up prices. His monopoly is no sooner effected than the peas in his storage barn swell and burst their bounds, bearing the broken shed atop their green, lava-like flood. The scene resembles the novel's ambiguous ending because it offers a "moonshine" version of Fraser's acquisitiveness that will be offset by the successful profiteering from nature's awesome fecundity.

The pigeon hunt indicates Fraser's entrepreneurial capacities. His search for the scientific mastery of the universe ends in wreckage, but his questing spirit and single-mindedness award him economic triumph. His mastery of the secret of capitalism — it is not the prospector who gets the gold, but the man who sells him shovels, tents and whiskey — gains him his mansion. He has a creative response to disaster — he turns a pigeon hunt into a harvest. He is one of the absent-minded makers of the new society.

A number of narrative motifs heighten the reader's sense of the new language and imagery Fraser seeks to master. At times directly, at time obliquely, through minor detail and major motif, the fabric of the technological society is synthesized. One tavern Fraser visits is called the Frozen Ocean. The talk in the bar conveys an atmosphere that is scientific-rational, republican and liberal; conversations describe a welter of new ideas and projects that will occupy the energies an increasingly secularist culture has released. Later in the story, Fraser hears a popular ballad about the doomed voyage of Sir John Franklin and the loss of him and his crew in the wastes of the frozen ocean. Franklin's search for the Northwest Passage, an incident in the march of exploration, offers a blend of science and romantic adventure, the sort of thing that occupies the talk of the tavern's customers.[14] Finally, he and his daughter twice view their land as a frozen ocean. The dream has come true.

Another motif is introduced at the beginning of the novel, when Fraser discovers the skeleton of a mastodon. The skeleton is articulated and trucked about the province. (Gibson writes that he based the story on an actual incident in the region where he farms.) The skeleton provides the beginnings of Fraser's rise. Gibson also describes the skeleton of a giant iguanodon that stood in London's Crystal Palace during the Great Exhibition of 1851. On one festive occasion, dinner was served to twenty-one guests in the belly of the reconstructed beast. What began as science concludes as circus, a thrilling wonder story that forms part of the folklore of industrial man.[15] It is part of the same spirit that will later produce science fiction or, as its greatest early practitioner called it, "scientific romance."

In this novel, Gibson combines romance, in the erotic sense, with science. Fraser's reveries lead from elephant bones to circus elephants to the show-girls who ride them. He masturbates to one show-girl's image. The dry bones lead to dreams of romance, adventure and sexual dominance. They are part of the solace science offers Fraser. The skeleton served its purpose in the protagonist's rise, and the dreaming of the bones concludes when one bone is inserted into a pivotal position in the contraption for perpetual motion. The great smash sends the bone flying. Fraser vows that his search will continue.

Gibson's novel demonstrates how far the historical novel has come and yet how traditional it remains. Gibson has worked for cultural nationalism and was chairman of the Writers' Union of Canada; his mention of nationalistic concerns should come as no surprise.[16] He speaks about the post-colonial need to reclaim our past and accommodate it imaginatively. Gibson's comments upon his novel's significance to the process of cultural redefinition describe an extra-literary motive for the historical novel's resurgence. It it easy to lose historical perspective on the possibilities for cultural nationalism while focussing on the defects and follies of the present.[17] A wide audience now exists for any examination of our past. The novels I discuss in this chapter appeared after the wave of nationalism that surged in the sixties. Much of that wave has receded, but some of our most serious writers have chosen as a subject the imaginative depiction of our past. Such an interest did not mark their other works.

But the best historical novels are not uncritical celebrations of accommodation and mastery. For example, *The Wars* shows the grounds for nationalism undermined by the destruction of people who can no longer survive in the culture they sought to preserve. Unlike *Five Legs* (1969) and *Communion* (1971), Gibson's historical novel is accessible. It is crammed with tall tale, irony, parody and comic incident.[18] Yet its message is a chilling one. Robert Fraser's triumph on its own terms is complete. In building his noble house, Fraser hews away the great oak that blocks the site he has chosen. He utters a prophecy — "There'll be Frasers here when this goddam forest and all these trees are gone!" — but which ironically does not convey the image of triumph he wants it to.

At times, the work may appear too close to being an imaginative diagram of an anti-modern ideology. But it also includes an earthy evocation of a rural culture's jobs and sayings. This lifts the weightiness from the reader. The novel demonstrates that, while nationalist concerns still occupy the attention of historical novelists, the specific nature of those concerns has altered. *Perpetual Motion* proclaims the triumph of a spirit with no qualms about that spirit's power to assimilate every potential contradictory and subversive impulse into the new order it has established. Gibson's reclamation of the past emphasizes wrong turnings and roads not taken. That subject also attracts Rudy Wiebe.

VI

Wiebe's novel *The Temptations of Big Bear* is ultimately a book about language. It is an imaginatively painstaking account of the killings at Frog Lake in 1885, of the context in which they occurred and of the role played by the great chief of the Plains Cree. The grounds for the conflict between Indians and whites were literal: land, space, living room. Wiebe's novel illustrates how some of these grounds are caught in language that expresses the divergent drives, which must clash. The language of the whites is abstract, and smashes head-on into the concreteness of the Cree language. Big Bear is indicted for offenses against the queen's "crown and dignity." He is puzzled and answers that "there is nothing true when they say I tried to steal her hat."[19] Such conflict symbolizes the conflicts between abstraction and concreteness that absorb the novel. Even views of the landscape conflict. The Cree are first seen as circular patterns that serve as a part of the land itself: "the Indians circled before him seemed not so much human as innumerable mounds the earth had thrust up since morning." The whites are associated with rectilinearity, with the grids on the surveyors' maps and the unyielding straightnesses of the railway line.

Big Bear has been the subject of considerable critical commentary. Critics have discussed its fidelity to history, its sophisticated use of narrative convention and its skilled blend of history and mythology.[20] Little remains to be said about the novel's technique; instead, I will concentrate on the book as historical fiction. I will begin by noting that the book does not present any easy moral judgements.[21]

To the white people who moved west, the Cree culture was an alien form. The Cree way of ordering society was so radically different that whites could come to terms with it only by changing it. Yet to change the Cree culture is to kill it. To accommodate the Cree culture or to restrain itself from using any portion of the technological might it possessed would violate the white culture's sense of itself; the white culture could not be expected to transcend its own norms of behaviour. Should the whites have learned a new language? They could not forgo their predatory drives any more than the Cree could have voluntarily quit the buffalo hunt.

Some people who read Wiebe's novel are slow to realize that the white man's "side" in the struggle is as alien to them as the Cree's. The novel does not let us make easy judgements. In colloquial speech, we often use the term "tragic" when we mean "inevitable." The Civil War or World War One we call tragic because we have the sense of vast, uncontrollable forces lumbering toward collision along unshiftable paths. The patterns of imagery, the circular motifs, the assured consciousnesses of the whites and the reminiscent and tentative consciousness of the Cree point to the kind of inevitability such use of the word "tragic" implies. Wiebe gives each narrative voice its own, true, peculiar pitch; the voices cease to be abstract and representative. They take on the weight — and the fumbling accident-proneness — of individuals.

The novel also contains tragedy in its technical sense. Big Bear begins as a revered, militant leader of his people; he becomes an old man who must watch as the Cree slaughter a group of whites Big Bear tried to protect.[22] The "temptations" of the title are never explicitly stated, but Big Bear is tempted to act when action would be inappropriate, to curse fate rather than submit to it, to justify himself rather than endure. These are the temptations Big Bear avoids. His final courtroom speech is a lament rather than an excoriation of his captors or an apology. The lament offers the nobler message and sustains Big Bear's tragic grandeur.

By his death, Big Bear enters the pantheon of Canadian heroes defined by their capacity to suffer and endure. Big Bear's endurance extends beyond the grave: "Slowly, slowly, all changed continually into indistinguishable, as it seemed, and everlasting, unchanging, rock." Wiebe does not ask us to weep at Big Bear's fate. We cannot ignore the claims Big Bear makes upon our sympathy, but neither should our sympathy cause us to choose sides.

Wiebe is careful not to bestow unwarranted grace or favour on any of his characters, Cree or white. An example of his wariness is found in a scene between the hero and his white captive, Kitty McLean. The sexual act is part of a larger process in which Big Bear tells Kitty a fable that foretells his apotheosis. In this episode Wiebe departs from historical sources; in the scene, the language barrier is vaulted by the act of love. For a moment, an abiding, rock-like humanity joins the two, who represent cultures in conflict. A single Indian and a single white person reach understanding and acceptance.

Big Bear calls on its readers to mourn and thus recovers a lost view of the past. The events of the novel were not lost in fact, but in imagination. Wiebe has written an alternative, losers' history; it is not a piece of contemporary polemic, and it is more demanding than polemical fiction, which would leave a sympathetic reader with the feeling that the good (that is, his) side lost. Tragedy demands contemplation and mourning; readers are again shown a mysterious, cosmic moral progress.

Wiebe's next novel, *The Scorched-Wood People* (1977), lacks the power of *Big Bear*.[23] *Big Bear* is full of narrative marvels; the reader is dazzled by the virtuousity of the many narrative voices — the anonymous Upper Canadian volunteer, the youthful Cree, the civil servant, Big Bear himself. The accounts are convincing, and each adds to the story in a particular way. This depth of vision yields to breadth in *The Scorched-Wood People*. The book is about Riel and the Métis. Wiebe's treatment of Riel and his visions demands a thoughtful and complex response from the reader, for the visions burn with conviction and compel the attention (and ambivalence) normal people give to prophetic utterance. But as Riel is speaking, Wiebe is also trying to advance the action. The result is jarring. Perhaps epic heroes should not be as introspective as Riel; prose fiction may be incapable of handling such diverse material in a single tone.

In *The Scorched-Wood People*, the polemical lines are too apparent; virtues and vices are too easily assignable to particular "sides." Wiebe uses a partisan narrator, the Métis balladeer Pierre Falcon. This could have proven an inspired choice, yet in the end the reader is given a one-sided version of events. We react rather than contemplate. One critic says that *The Scorched-Wood People* is superior to *The Temptations of Big Bear*: "The Métis . . . are presented uncritically, and the kind of complex cultural judgement we find in the earlier book is missing here."[24] That "complex cultural judgement" and the burden it places on the reader is *Big Bear*'s strength. In his historical fiction, Wiebe evokes the feel of a heroic age in which epic and tragedy were still possible. One Canadian historian called Big Bear "a little, ugly, proud-spirited man."[25] As Wiebe describes him, though, he is the stuff of tragedy. A sense of moral grandeur tells readers that these books are another brand of history, one readers are not used to. The familiar secular, materialist history is there, but it is surrounded by the nimbus of sacred history. In the most interesting portions of *The Scorched-Wood People*, Riel finds no contradiction between a reinterpretation of the entire course of the history of the Church of Rome and a concern for some people in danger of being shot to pieces at Duck Lake.[26] Big Bear is at once the tormented loser and the figure who will recede into the rock formations that dot his landscape. Wiebe's historical fiction is, at its best, at once traditional and radical, as in *The Temptations of Big Bear*. The result is the vision that humanity's greatness extends beyond materiality. Wiebe finds in our history a vision of human heroism that the world thought lost.

What of the nationalistic implications of Wiebe's historical fiction? In Timothy Findley's *The Wars*, the world of institutions and collective life cannot be discerned because of the insistent claims made by the personal and the elemental. Is Wiebe's world similar? Wiebe has dealt with the losers. In a slight novel, *The Mad Trapper* (1980), the violent loner eludes his pursuers by creating incomprehensible trails that loop back upon themselves. What do readers find in *The Temptations of Big Bear* and *The Scorched-Wood People*? Sadness at the sight of lost alternatives, exhilaration at the richness of our history. Contemplating what is not broadens our vision of what is. This is not nostalgia, for how can a modern white audience experience nostalgia over a process that was never its own? Instead, the audience is learning, listening to voices speak of dreams the audience never shared. Readers begin to evaluate their own dreams in the light of those alien dreams.

At present, Wiebe's historical novels stand as the culmination of the course of the Canadian historical novel. There are several reasons for the current flourishing of the historical novel. Better writers are beginning to use historical material; readers are more receptive to stories that heighten their sense of place. As well, historical novels are now providing critical and challenging versions of our history. They are bringing the Canadian historical novel back to the beginnings of the genre, the hard-headed evocation of defeated societies that marks the fiction of Sir Walter Scott. Finally, historical fiction is being written by experienced writers who have written in other genres. Creating good fiction from historical material is a challenge to good writers.

This seems clear from the work of one novelist. Peter Such's *Riverrun* (1973) has for its subject the last days of the Beothuck Indians of Newfoundland. These were the people who smeared themselves with red ochre and thus served as the excuse for the misnomer with which whites came to term all Amerindians. The semi-conscious, dream-filled narrative throws the reader into an alien experience and, in its brief pages, conveys a sense of the Beothuks' extinction and the white peoples' indifference. Such's other work ranges from contemporary novels to learned discussions of Canadian music; his historical excursion is novel. On the other hand, James Houston, a seasoned practitioner, cannot avoid the tired conventions of adventure fiction in his *The White Dawn* (1971), *Ghost Fox* (1977) and *Eagle Song* (1983). His near-contemporary *Spirit Wrestler* (1980) offers more satisfaction as a novel. While the fiction of Such and Houston is not as vital as Wiebe's, all of their historical works belong to the same project. What the Bible does for the Judeo-Christian tradition, historical fiction and history provide for the yearnings of secular man. The presentation of dead ends and lost causes must be included in that progress. The fiction of roads not taken serves ultimately a contemplative function. The triumphalist fiction of the nineteenth century — such works as *The Golden Dog* and *The Seats of the Mighty* — include a note of warning: "Corruption destroyed these past societies; it could destroy ours too." Yet the total course of these novels is triumphal. A new order follows the old, and melds together the best of both. Novels of the middle period presented images of accommodation — either to the demands of a New World environment or (in the case of French-Canadian fiction) to the facts of a historical experience more complex than that of epic heroism going down in defeat. The present period culminates in Wiebe because he adds feature of his own to the formal and thematic innovation that marks other current novelists: the return to the chronicle of magnificence, the celebration of truly remarkable persons and deeds. Yet such grandeur did not fall on the winning side. Wiebe's tales place before the reader a complex reality that yields to no easy moralizing. Wiebe's finest critic notes, almost in passing, that "serious historical fiction does not yet form a prominent part of Canadian literature."[27] The works studied here should put that statement to rest. The genre has begun to attract our best writers; to chart the outlines of the journey from the beginning has been this essay's task.

NOTES

[1] In order of publication, see Albert Le Grand, "'Kamouraska' ou l'Ange et la Bête," *Etudes Francaises*, 7 (fev. 1971), 119–43; Adrien Thério, "La maison de la belle et du prince ou l'enfer dans l'oeuvre romanesque d'Anne Hébert," *Livres et Auteurs Québecois*, 1971, pp. 274–84; Margot Northey, *The Haunted Wilderness*, pp. 53–61; E. D. Blodgett, "Prisms and Arcs: Structures in Hébert and Munro," in Diane Bessai and David Jackel, eds., *Figures in a Ground. Canadian Essays on Modern Literature Collected in Honor of Shiela Watson* (Saskatoon: Western

Producer Prairie Books, 1978) pp. 99–121; John Lennox, "Dark Journeys: *Kamouraska* and *Deliverance*," *Essays on Canadian Writing*, No. 12 (Fall 1978), pp. 84–104; Barbara Godard, "My (m)Other, My Self: Strategies for Subversion in Atwood and Hébert," *Essays on Canadian Writing*, No. 26 (Summer 1983), pp. 13–44.

2 Many critics discuss narcissism, madness, windows, mirrors and interior monologues; many also refer readers to an article on the historicity of the *crime passionnel*. For more on the historicity, see Françoise M. Defresne, "Le Drame de Kamouraska," *Québec-Histoire*, vol. 1 (Juin-Aôut 1972), pp. 22–27.

3 This aspect of the novel is discussed in the article "Dark Journeys" by John Lennox, noted above.

4 I cannot understand why the translator changed this to " 'It's that damned woman. She's ruined me . . . . ' "

5 Donald Smith, "Jacques Ferron," in William Toye, ed., *The Oxford Companion to Canadian Literature* (Toronto: Oxford Univ. Press, 1983), pp. 254–55.

6 "Robert Ross came to me whole; he came, as people have often said, because of the technique, letters, and people's remembrances and so on, as if he had been real." Johan Aitken, " 'Long Live the Dead': an Interview with Timothy Findley," *Journal of Canadian Fiction*, No. 33 (1981–82), p. 81.

7 See Paul Fussell, *The Great War and Modern Memory* (New York: Oxford Univ. Press, 1975); Eric Thompson, "Canadian Fiction of the Great War," *Canadian Literature*, No. 91 (Winter 1981), pp. 81–96; Dagmar Novak, "The Canadian Novel and the Two World Wars" (Diss. Toronto 1985).

8 Criticism of *The Wars* tends to settle largely around its narrative form and its "authenticity." See Eva-Marie Kröller, "The Exploding Frame: Uses of Photography in Timothy Findley's *The Wars*," *Journal of Canadian Studies*, 16, Nos. 3 and 4 (Autumn–Winter 1981), 68–74; Bruce Pirie, "The Dragon in the Fog: 'Displaced Mythology' in *The Wars*," *Canadian Literature*, No. 91 (Winter 1981), pp. 70–79; also in issue 91 of *Canadian Literature*, see articles by John F. Hulcoop, Peter Klovan, and Eric Thompson; Gilbert Drolet, " 'Prayers Against Despair': A Retrospective Note on Findley's *The Wars*," *Journal of Canadian Fiction*, No. 33 (1981–82), pp. 148–55.

9 The article by Drolet (see note 8) offers a military historian's support of the novel's authenticity.

10 Peter Allen, "Narrative Uncertainty in Duncan's *The Imperialist*," *Studies in Canadian Literature*, 9 (1984), 41n.

11 George Grant, "In Defense of North America," in his *Technology and Empire. Perspectives on North America* (Toronto: House of Anansi, 1969), pp. 23–25.

12 Graeme Gibson, "Gothic Shocks from History: The Birth of a New Novel," *The Globe and Mail*, 4 June 1983, p. E17. On the genesis of the novel, see also Geoff Hancock, "Interview with Graeme Gibson," *Books in Canada*, Nov. 1982, pp. 24–27.

13 Gibson, "Gothic Shocks."

14 While our culture is far from a seamless web, an interesting parallel with Gibson exists in the folk songs of the late Stan Rogers. His first album, *Fogarty's Cove* (Barn Swallow Records BS 1001), features "Barrett's Privateers," a song about a disastrous moment in a perennial Canadian turn-about dream, that of ripping off the Americans. This Fraser accomplishes when he exploits the needs of itinerant pigeon hunters from the United States. A later Rogers album, *North–West Passage* (Fogarty's Cove Music FCM 004) has for its title song a haunting refrain that recalls Sir John Franklin's voyage.

15 In fact, the dinner happened. Twenty-one people were seated inside the immense model of the beast's skeleton, while another seven dined at an adjoining table. The host was Mr. B. Waterhouse Hawkins. Sir Richard Owen (1804–92), the distinguished comparative anatomist and paleontologist who assembled the skeleton (and in whose honour the meal was given), has a further link with the novel. He provided notes for Captain Belcher's account of his search for the survivors of the Franklin Expedition. (Sir Edward Belcher, *The Last of the Arctic Voyages*, 2 vols. [London: L. Reeve, 1855].) As with Fraser's grand machine, Owen's labours at times exuded an air of the ridiculous. His biographer–grandson writes of visiting the display of giant skeletons decades after their unveiling at the Great Exhibition. By then, the labels had disappeared and an uncomprehending public speculated as to whether the objects were not a "terrible warning [of] the fantastic visions sometimes seen by such as are in the habit of indulging too freely in spirituous liquors." (Rev. Richard Startin Owen, *The Life of Richard Owen*. 2 vols [London: John Murray, 1894], I, p. 398n.)

16 "Latin American writers have the same post-colonial need that we have to reclaim the past, to find in it — or impose upon it — those more personal and immediate patterns that are essential if we are to make any sense of our present" ("Gothic Shocks"). "So much Latin-American literature is historical. In a post-colonial society, that's what you have to do. You have to go back and tell your history in a way that is meaningful to the people who actually live there" ("Interview," p. 27).

17 A corrective to this may be found in Robert Bothwell, Ian Drummond and John English, *Canada Since 1945: Power, Politics and Provincialism* (Toronto: Univ. of Toronto Press, 1981), pp. 332–37, 437–54.

18 Gibson's second novel anticipates *The Wars* both in its use of a single scene that recurs in word-for-word fashion, and in its hero's fatal quest for a reunion with the animal world as a search for the life we have denied.

19 This statement was actually made. Historians disagree, however, as to who said it, Big Bear or Little Arrow. For Big Bear, see Hugh A. Dempsey, *Big Bear: The End of Freedom* (Vancouver/Toronto: Douglas & McIntyre, 1984), pp. 74–76. For Little Arrow, see Bob Beal and Rod MacLeod, *Prairie Fire: The 1885 North-West Rebellion* (Edmonton: Hurtig, 1985), p. 309.

20 See Allen Ducek, "Rudy Wiebe's Approach to Historical Fiction: a Study of *The Temptations of Big Bear* and *The Scorched-Wood People*," in John Moss, ed., *The Canadian Novel: Here and Now* (Toronto: NC, 1978), pp. 182–99; Dick Harrison, *Unnamed Country: The Struggle for a Canadian Prairie Fiction* (Edmonton: Univ. of Alberta Press, 1977), pp. 200–04; W. J. Keith, *Epic Fiction: The Art of Rudy Wiebe* (Edmonton: Univ. of Alberta Press, 1981); W. J. Keith, ed., *A Voice in the Land: Essays By and About Rudy Wiebe* (Edmonton: NeWest, 1981), esp. essays by Redekop (pp. 97–123), Bilan (pp. 171–74), Solecki (pp. 175–78) and Jeffrey (pp. 179–201); Robert Lecker, "Twisting the Quintuplet Senses: Time and Form in *The Temptations of Big Bear*," *English Studies in Canada*, 8 (Sept. 1982), 333–48; Glenn Meeter, "Rudy Wiebe: Spatial Form and Christianity in *The Blue Mountains of China* and "*The Temptations of Big Bear*," *Essays on Canadian Writing*, No. 22 (Summer 1981), pp. 42–61; Leslie Monkman, *A Native Heritage: Images of the Indian in English-Canadian Literature* (Toronto: Univ. of Toronto Press, 1981), pp. 116–19; John Moss, *Sex and Violence in the Canadian Novel* (Toronto: McClelland and Stewart, 1977), pp. 256–73; Lauralyn Taylor, "*The Temptations of Big Bear*: A Filmic Novel?" *Essays on Canadian Writing*, No. 9 (Winter 1978), pp. 134–38.

21 I owe the germ of this idea to a conversation in 1980 with Professor Dick Harrison of the University of Alberta.

22 Wiebe, "On the Trail of Big Bear," in *Epic Fiction*, p. 134.

23 Such formidable critics of Wiebe's fiction as Keith and Solecki (see note 20) award this novel pride of place in his oeuvre, a judgement with which I cannot agree.

24 See Bilan in *Epic Fiction*, p. 173.

25 Desmond Morton, *The Last War Drum: The North West Campaign of 1885* (Toronto: Hakkert, 1972), p. 16.

26 The convincing nature of this duality makes *The Scorched-Wood People* a far richer work than Jean-Jules Richard's *Exovide Louis Riel* (Montréal: Editions La Presse, 1972).

27 W. J. Keith, *Epic Fiction*, p. 88.

BIBLIOGRAPHY

Caron, Louis. *Le canard de bois* (*Les fils de la liberté*, tome I). Montréal: Boréal Express, 1981.

——. *La corne de brume* (*Les fils de la liberté*, II). Québec: Boréal Express, 1982.

——. *L'emmitouflé*. Paris: Lafont, 1977. Trans. into English by David Toby Hamel as *The Draft Dodger*. Toronto: House of Anansi, 1980.

Caron, St.-Arnaud. *Vandeboncoeur* (*L'érable et le castor*, tome I). Paris: Acropole, 1983.

Ferron, Jacques. *Le Saint–Elias*. Montréal: Éditions du Jour, 1972. Trans. into English by Pierre Cloutier as *The Saint Elias*. Montreal: Harvest House, 1975.

———. *Le ciel de Québec*. 2nd ed. Montréal: Éditions du Jour, 1979. Trans. into English by Ray Ellenwood as *The Penniless Redeemer*. Toronto: Exile Editions, 1984.

Findley, Timothy. *The Wars*. Toronto: Clarke, Irwin, 1977.

Gibson, Graeme. *Perpetual Motion*. Toronto: McClelland and Stewart, 1982.

Gill, Stephen. *The Loyalist City*. Cornwall, Ont.: Vesta Publications, 1979.

Hébert, Anne. *Les Fous de Bassan*. Montréal: Éditions du Seuil, 1982. Trans. into English by Sheila Fischman as *In the Shadow of the Wind*. Toronto: Stoddart, 1983.

———. *Kamouraska*. Paris: Editions du Seuil, 1970. Trans. into English by Norman Shapiro as *Kamouraska*. Toronto: Musson, 1973.

Houston, James. *Eagle Song*. Toronto: McClelland and Stewart, 1983.

———. *Ghost Fox*. New York: Harcourt Brace Jovanovich, 1976.

———. *Spirit Wrestler*. Toronto: McClelland and Stewart, 1980.

———. *The White Dawn: An Eskimo Legend*. Toronto: Longmans, 1971.

Jack, Donald. *It's Me Again* Toronto: Doubleday, 1975.

———. *Me Bandy, You Cissie*. Toronto: Doubleday, 1979.

———. *Me Too*. Toronto: Doubleday, 1983.

———. *That's Me in the Middle*. Toronto: Doubleday, 1973.

———. *Three Cheers for Me*. Toronto: Macmillan, 1962.

Kevan, Martin. *Racing Tides*. Toronto: General, 1985.

Lamirande, Claire de. *Papineau ou l'épée à double tranchant*. Montréal: Les Quinze, 1980.

Laroque De Roquebrune, Robert. *La seigneuresse*. Montréal: Fides, 1960.

Maillet, Antonine. *Pélagie–La–Charrette*. Montréal: Grosset et Laméoc, 1979. Trans. into English by Philip Stratford as *Pélagie*. Toronto: Doubleday, 1982.

Moore, Brian. *Black Robe*. Toronto: McClelland and Stewart, 1985.

Richard, Jean–Jules. *Exovide Louis Riel*. Montréal: Editions La Presse, 1972.

Robertson, Heather. *Willie. A Romance* (Volume I of *The King Papers*) Toronto: James Lorimer, 1983.

Such, Peter. *Riverrun*. Toronto: Clarke, Irwin, 1973.

Wall, Robert E. *Birthright* (Book III of *The Canadians*). Toronto: Personal Library, 1982.

———. *Blackrobe* (Book I of *The Canadians*). Toronto: Personal Library, 1981.

———. *Bloodbrothers* (Book II of *The Canadians*). Toronto: Personal Library, 1981.

———. *Patriots* (Book IV of *The Canadians*). Toronto: NC, 1983.

Wiebe, Rudy. *The Scorched-Wood People*. Toronto: McClelland and Stewart, 1977.

———. *The Temptations of Big Bear*. Toronto: McClelland and Stewart, 1973.

Wright, Richard B. *Farthing's Fortunes*. Toronto: Macmillan, 1976.

York, Thomas. *Trapper*. New York: Doubleday, 1981.

INDEX

81